"Don't Forget to Sing in the Lifeboats."

UNCOMMON
WISDOM
for
UNCOMMON
TIMES

"Don't Forget to Sing in the Lifeboats."

by Kathryn & Ross Petras
with Illustrations by R. O. Blechman

WORKMAN PUBLISHING · NEW YORK

Library of Congress Cataloging-in-Publication Data is available.

ISBN 978-0-7611-5614-7

Workman books are available at special discounts when purchased
in bulk for premiums and sales promotions as well as for fund-
raising or educational use. Special editions or book excerpts can
also be created to specification. For details, contact the Special Sales
Director at the address below.

Workman Publishing Company, Inc.
225 Varick Street
New York, NY 10014-4381
www.workman.com

Printed in Singapore

First printing April 2009

10 9 8 7 6 5 4 3 2 1

Introduction

W orried about your pension? Your mortgage? Your job? Join the club! Thinking the future looks a little uncertain? Come on in! Feeling as if the pressure cooker of life is getting ready to cook your goose? Here, we'll make room for you . . .

That's the point: Whatever issues we're staring down, we are not alone. Indeed, throughout history people have lived in what felt like (and often were) uncommon times. What you hold in your hand is a collection of the insight and wit that helped many of those who came before us— as well as a few of our living poets and scholars, singers and statesmen—make it to the other side of difficulty.

This uncommon wisdom includes quotes from people who have been there, done that, and lived to tell the tale. People who have graduated from the school of hard knocks, yet kept a sense of perspective—and often a sense of humour. People who, like all of us, struggled to keep on keeping on . . . and usually did.

As the physicist Stephen Hawking once said, "Life would be tragic if it weren't funny." Or, as our title suggests, courtesy of Voltaire, "Life is a shipwreck, but we must not forget to sing in the lifeboats."

Kathryn and Ross Petras
New York City

Acceptance

Life is a crisis— so what!

—MALCOLM BRADBURY
Writer

The Fine Art of Being Happy

The point of living, and of being an optimist, is to be foolish enough to believe the best is yet to come.

— PETER USTINOV
Actor

Never Give Up

Never let your head hang down. Never give up and sit down and grieve. Find another way. And don't pray when it rains if you don't pray when the sun shines.

— LEROY "SATCHEL" PAIGE
Baseball player

Money

October. This is one of the peculiarly dangerous months to speculate in stocks in. The others are July, January, September, April, November, May, March, June, December, August, and February.

—MARK TWAIN
Writer

True Grit

He who loses wealth loses much. He who loses a friend loses more. But he that loses his courage loses all.

— MIGUEL DE CERVANTES
Writer

Perseverance

It even helps stupid people
to try hard.

—LUCIUS ANNAEUS SENECA
Philosopher

It's How You Look at Things

If you think you have it
tough, read history books.

—BILL MAHER
Comedian

How to Live

Have courage for the great sorrows of life and patience for the small ones; and when you have laboriously accomplished your daily task, go to sleep in peace. God is awake.

— VICTOR HUGO
Writer

Taking Action

The first step towards getting somewhere is to decide that you are not going to stay where you are.

—J. P. MORGAN
Financier

Problems, Problems

For every problem there is a solution which is simple, clean and wrong.

—H. L. MENCKEN
Journalist

Success and Failure

Ninety-nine percent of the failures come from people who have the habit of making excuses.

—George Washington Carver
Scientist and Inventor

The Silver Lining

When one's expectations are reduced to zero, one really appreciates everything one does have.

—STEPHEN HAWKING
Physicist

You Might As Well Laugh

I know God will not give me anything I can't handle. I just wish that He didn't trust me so much.

—MOTHER TERESA
Humanitarian

Secrets of Getting Ahead

Work hard, keep your mouth shut, and answer your mail.

— THOMAS J. PENDERGAST
Political boss of Kansas City,
giving advice to Harry S Truman
when he was leaving to serve
his first term in the Senate

Truths

It's the great mystery of human life that old grief passes gradually into quiet tender joy.

— FYODOR DOSTOEVSKY
Writer

Survival Tactics

Drag your thoughts
away from your
troubles . . . by the
ears, by the heels,
or any other way you
can manage it.

— MARK TWAIN
Writer

Facing Life Head-On

Life's a bitch. You've got to go out and kick ass.

—MAYA ANGELOU
Writer

Hope

As long as there is one upright man, as long as there is one compassionate woman, the contagion may spread and the scene is not desolate. Hope is the one thing left to us in a bad time.

—E. B. WHITE
Writer

Rules to Live By

The first rule of holes: when you're in one, stop digging.

—MOLLY IVINS
Writer

Counting Your Blessings

I consider myself blessed.
I consider you blessed.
We've all been blessed with
God-given talents. Mine
just happens to be beating
people up.

—SUGAR RAY LEONARD
Boxer

Coping

Sorrow can be alleviated by good sleep, a bath and a glass of wine.

—THOMAS AQUINAS
Philosopher

Try, Try Again

Do not be too timid and squeamish about your actions. All life is an experiment. The more experiments you make the better. What if they are a little coarse, and you may get your coat soiled or torn? What if you do fail, and get fairly rolled in the dirt once or twice. Up again, you shall never be so afraid of a tumble.

— RALPH WALDO EMERSON
Essayist and Philosopher

The Right Attitude

Fear tastes like a rusty knife and do not let her into your house.

—JOHN CHEEVER
Writer

Eat, Drink, and Be Merry

Life is uncertain.
Eat dessert first.

—ERNESTINE ULMER
Writer

Testing Yourself

People are like stained glass windows: They sparkle and shine when the sun's out, but when the darkness sets in, their true beauty is revealed only if there is light within.

—ELIZABETH KÜBLER-ROSS
Doctor and Thanatologist

Friends

Q. How do you define friendship?

Investor WARREN BUFFETT:

A. I remember asking that question of a woman who had survived Auschwitz. She said her test was, "Would they hide me?"

The Silver Lining

There is much to be said for failure. It is more interesting than success.

— MAX BEERBOHM
Parodist and Caricaturist

Life Goes On

Whatever tears one may shed, in the end one always blows one's nose.

—HEINRICH HEINE
Writer

Things I've Learned

Life is tough, but it's tougher when you're stupid.

—John Wayne
Actor

Living on Less

Now is no time to think
of what you do not have.
Think of what you can do
with what there is.

— ERNEST HEMINGWAY
Writer

Balance

Sooner or later in life everyone discovers that perfect happiness is unrealizable, but there are few who pause to consider the antithesis: that perfect unhappiness is equally unattainable.

—PRIMO LEVI
Chemist and Writer

Coping

Is your cucumber bitter? Throw it away. Are there briars in your path? Turn aside. That is enough. Do not go on to say, "Why were things of this sort ever brought into this world?"

—MARCUS AURELIUS
Roman emperor and Philosopher

It's How You Look at Things

I've never been poor, only broke. Being poor is a frame of mind. Being broke is only a temporary situation.

—MIKE TODD
Film producer

Self-Worth

I cannot think that we are useless or God would not have created us.

—GERONIMO
Apache leader

Perseverance

Only entropy comes easy.

—LEWIS MUMFORD
Urban historian

Survival Tactics

When you're at the end of your rope, all you have to do is make one foot move out in front of the other. Just take the next step. That's all there is to it.

—SAMUEL FULLER
Film director

The Silver Lining

If the skies fall, one may hope to catch larks.

—FRANÇOIS RABELAIS
Writer

Faith

Life is a gamble. You can get hurt, but people die in plane crashes, lose their arms and legs in car accidents; people die every day. Same with fighters: some die, some get hurt, some go on. You just don't let yourself believe it will happen to you.

—MUHAMMAD ALI
Boxer

Taking Action

An ant on the move does more than a dozing ox.

—LAO-TZU
Philosopher

Rules to Live By

Don't believe the world owes you a living; the world owes you nothing— it was here first.

—ROBERT JONES BURDETTE
Clergyman and Journalist

Don't Worry, Be Happy

Life is a shipwreck, but we must not forget to sing in the lifeboats.

—FRANÇOIS-MARIE
AROUET VOLTAIRE
Philosopher and Writer

Acceptance

If a ship has been sunk, I can't bring it up. If it is going to be sunk, I can't stop it. I can use my time much better working on tomorrow's problem than by fretting about yesterday's. Besides, if I let those things get me, I wouldn't last long.

—ERNEST J. KING
Admiral

Never Give Up

Pain is temporary. It may last a minute, or an hour, or a day, or a year, but eventually it will subside and something else will take its place. If I quit, however, it lasts forever.

—LANCE ARMSTRONG
Cyclist

Money

Why is there so much month left at the end of the money?

—JOHN BARRYMORE
Actor

The Fine Art of Being Happy

Happiness is a how, not a what; a talent, not an object.

—HERMANN HESSE
Writer

True Grit

Ho-ka hey! It is a good day to fight! It is a good day to die! Strong hearts, brave hearts to the front! Weak hearts and cowards to the rear!

—CRAZY HORSE
Oglala Sioux chief

It's How You Look at Things

The long run is a misleading guide to current affairs. In the long run we are all dead.

—JOHN MAYNARD KEYNES
Economist

How to Live

Expect nothing. Live frugally on surprise.

—ALICE WALKER
Writer

Taking Action

For those who are willing
to make an effort, great
miracles and wonderful
treasures are in store.

— Issac Bashevis Singer
Writer

Problems, Problems

If you see ten troubles coming down the road, you can be sure that nine will run into the ditch before they reach you.

—CALVIN COOLIDGE
U.S. President

Success and Failure

We are all of us failures—
at least, the best of us are.

—J. M. BARRIE
Playwright and Novelist

Schubert's
Unfinished
Symphony

The Silver Lining

Do you not see
how necessary
a world of pains and
troubles is to school
an intelligence and
make it a soul?

—JOHN KEATS
Poet

The Fine Art of Being Happy

Men can only be happy when they do not assume that the object of life is happiness.

—GEORGE ORWELL
Writer

The Silver Lining

Do you not see how necessary a world of pains and troubles is to school an intelligence and make it a soul?

—JOHN KEATS
Poet

The Fine Art of Being Happy

Men can only be happy when they do not assume that the object of life is happiness.

—George Orwell
Writer

Truths

Nobody is always a winner, and anybody who says he is, is either a liar or doesn't play poker.

— AMARILLO SLIM
Poker player

Facing Life Head-On

When a resolute young fellow steps up to the great bully, the world, and takes him boldly by the beard, he is often surprised to find it comes off in his hand, and that it was only tied on to scare away the timid adventurers.

— RALPH WALDO EMERSON
Essayist and Philosopher

Faith

I have noticed even people
who claim everything is
predestined, and that we
can do nothing to change
it, look before they cross
the road.

—STEPHEN HAWKING
Physicist

Rules to Live By

Don't ever forget two things I'm going to tell you. One, don't believe everything that's written about you. Two, don't pick up too many checks.

—BABE RUTH
Baseball player

What Really Matters

So give to the poor; I'm begging you, I'm warning you, I'm commanding you, I'm ordering you.

—St. Augustine of Hippo
Philosopher and Theologian

Coping

In times like these it is good to remember that there have always been times like these.

—PAUL HARVEY
Radio broadcaster

The Right Attitude

My attitude is never to be satisfied, never enough, never.

— DUKE ELLINGTON
Musician

Eat, Drink, and Be Merry

When men drink, then they are rich and successful and win lawsuits and are happy and help their friends. Quickly, bring me a beaker of wine, so that I may wet my mind and say something clever.

— ARISTOPHANES
Playwright

Testing Yourself

It is easy to be independent when you've got money. But to be independent when you haven't got a thing— that's the Lord's test.

— MAHALIA JACKSON
Singer

Money

Why does a slight tax
increase cost you two
hundred dollars and a
substantial tax cut save
you thirty cents?

— PEG BRACKEN
Writer

Perseverance

Look at a stone cutter hammering away at his rock, perhaps a hundred times without as much as a crack showing in it. Yet at the hundred-and-first blow it will split in two, and I know it was not the last blow that did it, but all that had gone before.

—Jacob A. Riis
Journalist and Photographer

Things I've Learned

People who boast about their IQ are losers.

—STEPHEN HAWKING
Physicist

Living on Less

If you don't get everything you want, think of the things you don't get that you don't want.

—OSCAR WILDE
Writer

Balance

Remember that there is nothing stable in human affairs; therefore avoid undue elation in prosperity, or undue depression in adversity.

—SOCRATES
Philosopher

Grace Under Pressure

It is always in the midst, in the epicenter, of your troubles that you find serenity.

—ANTOINE DE SAINT-EXUPÉRY
Writer and Pilot

Life Lessons

I'll never make that mistake again, reading the experts' opinions. Of course, you only live one life, and you make all your mistakes, and learn what not to do, and that's the end of you.

— RICHARD FEYNMAN
Physicist

Self-Worth

And above all things, never think that you're not good enough yourself. A man should never think that. My belief is that in life people will take you at your own reckoning.

—ISAAC ASIMOV
Writer

Survival Tactics

When you have got an elephant by the hind legs and he is trying to run away, it's best to let him run.

— ABRAHAM LINCOLN
U.S. President

The Silver Lining

You may not realize it when it happens, but a kick in the teeth may be the best thing in the world for you.

— Walt Disney
Film producer and Director

Fighting Back

If there is no struggle there is no progress. Those who profess to favor freedom and yet depreciate agitation . . . want crops without plowing up the ground, they want rain without thunder and lightning. They want the ocean without the awful roar of its many waters. . . . Power concedes nothing without a demand. It never did and it never will.

—FREDERICK DOUGLASS
Abolitionist and Activist

Rules to Live By

Rule Number One:
Never lose money.
Rule Number Two:
Never forget rule
Number One.

—WARREN BUFFETT
Investor

Don't Worry, Be Happy

Nobody really cares if you're miserable, so you might as well be happy.

—CYNTHIA NELMS
Writer

Acceptance

The best thing one can do when it's raining is to let it rain.

—HENRY WADSWORTH LONGFELLOW
Writer

The Fine Art of Being Happy

Be content with what you have; rejoice in the way things are. When you realize there is nothing lacking, the whole world belongs to you.

—LAO-TZU
Philosopher

Never Give Up

Hard times ain't quit and
we ain't quit.

—MERIDEL LE SUEUR
Writer and Activist

Money

The fundamental evil of the
world arose from the fact
that the good Lord has not
created money enough.

—HEINRICH HEINE
Writer

True Grit

At times of distress,
strengthen your
heart.
Even if you stand at
death's door.
The lamp has light
before it is
extinguished.
The wounded lion still
knows how to roar.

—SAMUEL HANAGID
Poet

How to Live

So live your life that the fear of death can never enter your heart. Trouble no one about their religion; respect others in their view, and demand that they respect yours. Love your life, perfect your life, beautify all things in your life. Seek to make your life long and its purpose in the service of your people.

Prepare a noble death song for the day when you go over the great divide. Always give a word or a sign of salute when meeting or passing a friend, even a stranger, when in a lonely place. Show respect to all people and grovel to none. When you arise in the morning give thanks for the food and for the joy of living. If you see no reason for giving thanks, the fault lies only in yourself.

Abuse no one and no thing, for abuse turns the wise ones to fools and robs the spirit of its vision. When it comes your time to die, be not like those whose hearts are filled with the fear of death, so that when their time comes they weep and pray for a little more time to live their lives over again in a different way. Sing your death song and die like a hero going home.

— TECUMSEH
Shawnee chief
(also sometimes attributed to AUPUMUT
Mohican chief)

We All Make Mistakes

As long as the world is turning and spinning, we're gonna be dizzy and we're gonna make mistakes.

—MEL BROOKS
Film director, Comedian, and Producer

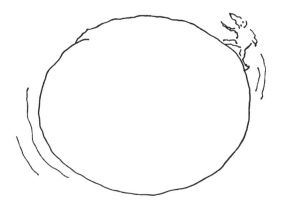

Taking Action

Get action.
Seize the moment.
Man was never
intended to become
an oyster.

— THEODORE ROOSEVELT
U.S. President

Problems, Problems

When you don't have any money, the problem is food. When you have money, it's sex. When you have both, it's health. If everything is simply jake, then you're frightened of death.

—J. P. DONLEAVY
Writer

Success and Failure

You gotta lose 'em some of the time. When you do, lose 'em right.

—CASEY STENGEL
Baseball manager

The Silver Lining

Adversities do not make a man frail. They show what sort of man he is.

—THOMAS À KEMPIS
Mystic

An Ironic Twist

I don't consider myself a pessimist. I think of a pessimist as someone who is waiting for it to rain. And I feel soaked to the skin.

—LEONARD COHEN
Singer and Songwriter

Secrets of Getting Ahead

Always have a vivid imagination, for you never know when you might need it.

—J. K. ROWLING
Writer

Facing Life Head-On

The hottest places
in Hell are reserved
for those who in
time of great moral
crises maintain their
neutrality.

—DANTE ALIGHIERI
Poet

Rules to Live By

Don't gamble; take all your savings and buy some good stock and hold it till it goes up, then sell it. If it don't go up, don't buy it.

—WILL ROGERS
Humorist

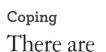

Coping

There are
two means

of refuge from the miseries
of life: music and cats.

— ALBERT SCHWEITZER
Humanitarian and Philosopher

Try, Try Again

If at first you don't succeed, try, try again. Then quit. There's no use being a damn fool about it.

—W. C. FIELDS
Actor and Comedian

The Right Attitude

Pessimism is, in brief, playing the sure game. You cannot lose at it; you may gain. It is the only view of life in which you can never be disappointed. Having reckoned what to do in the worst possible circumstances, when better arise, as they may, life becomes child's play.

—Thomas Hardy
Writer

Eat, Drink, and Be Merry

If you lose the power to laugh, you lose the power to think.

—CLARENCE DARROW
Lawyer

Testing Yourself

You can't test courage cautiously.

—ANNIE DILLARD
Writer

Friends

Grant stood by me when I was crazy, and I stood by him when he was drunk, and now we stand by each other.

—WILLIAM T. SHERMAN
U.S. Civil War general

Money

I do want to get rich but I never want to do what there is to do to get rich.

—GERTRUDE STEIN
Writer

Life Goes On

Despite everybody who has been born and has died, the world has just gone on. I mean, look at Napoleon—but we went right on. Look at Harpo Marx—the world went around, it didn't stop for a second. It's sad but true. John Kennedy, right?

—BOB DYLAN
Musician

Things I've Learned

Not everything that can be counted counts, and not everything that counts can be counted.

— ALBERT EINSTEIN
Physicist

Living on Less

The day, water, sun, moon, night—I do not have to purchase these things with money.

—TITUS MACCIUS PLAUTUS
Playwright

Truths

Whatever you may be sure of, be sure of this: that you are dreadfully like other people.

— JAMES RUSSELL LOWELL
Editor and Writer

Coping

If you suppress grief too much, it can well redouble.

— MOLIÈRE
(JEAN-BAPTISTE POQUELIN)
Playwright

We All Make Mistakes

Success is relative. It is what we can make of the mess we have made of things.

— T.S. ELIOT
Writer

Self-Worth

Never forget that you are one of a kind. Never forget that if there weren't any need for you in all your uniqueness to be on this earth, you wouldn't be here in the first place. And never forget, no matter how overwhelming life's challenges and problems seem to be, that one person can make a difference in the world. In fact, it is always because of one person that all the changes that matter in the world come about. So be that one person.

—R. BUCKMINSTER FULLER
Philosopher

Survival Tactics

L ook at misfortune the
same way you look
at success: Don't panic.
Do your best and forget
the consequences.

— WALTER ALSTON
Baseball manager

Tongue in Cheek

Time for belt-tightening.
You can't live on a million
a year anymore.

—RANDY NEWMAN
Musician

Fighting Back

Look now, my brother, the white people think we have no brains in our heads, but that they are great and big; and that makes them make war with us. We are but a little handful to what you are, but remember . . . when you hunt for a rattlesnake, you cannot find it, and perhaps it will bite you before you see it.

—SHINGIS
Delaware chief

Secrets of Getting Ahead

It's not the will to win that matters— everyone has that. It's the will to prepare to win that matters.

—BEAR BRYANT
Football coach

Rules to Live By

Make it a rule of life never to regret and never to look back. Regret is an appalling waste of energy; you can't build on it; it's only for wallowing in.

—KATHERINE MANSFIELD
Writer

Hope

He that lives upon hope, dies farting.

—BENJAMIN FRANKLIN
Statesman

Don't Worry, Be Happy

Don't take life too seriously. It ain't nohow permanent.

—WALT KELLY
Cartoonist

Acceptance

Rivers know this:
There is no hurry.
We shall get there.

— A. A. MILNE
Writer

The Fine Art of Being Happy

The secret to being miserable is to have leisure to bother about whether you are happy or not.

—GEORGE BERNARD SHAW
Playwright

Never Give Up

My motto was always to keep swinging. Whether I was in a slump or feeling badly or having trouble off the field, the only thing to do was keep swinging.

—HANK AARON
Baseball player

Money

Making money ain't nothing exciting to me. You might be able to buy a little better booze than the wino on the corner. But you get sick just like the next cat and when you die you're just as graveyard dead as he is.

—LOUIS ARMSTRONG
Musician

It's How You Look at Things

You walk through a series of arches, so to speak, and then, presently, at the end of a corridor, a door opens and you see backward through time, and you feel the flow of time, and realize you are only part of a great nameless procession.

—JOHN HUSTON
Film director

How to Live

Waste no more time arguing what a good man should be. Be one.

—MARCUS AURELIUS
Roman emperor and Philosopher

Taking Action

How do you know what you're going to do until you do it? The answer is, you don't. It's a stupid question.

—J. D. SALINGER
Writer

It's How You Look at Things

Problems are not the problem; coping is the problem.

— Virginia Satir
Psychologist and Educator

Success and Failure

Notice the difference between what happens when a man says to himself, "I have failed three times," and what happens when he says, "I am a failure."

—S. I. HAYAKAWA
U.S. Senator and Semanticist

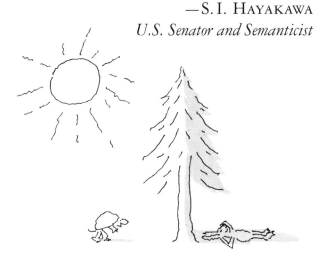

The Silver Lining

The world breaks everyone and afterward many are stronger at the broken places.

—ERNEST HEMINGWAY
Writer

Laughter

Generally speaking, the poorer person summers where he winters.

— FRAN LEBOWITZ
Humorist

Secrets of Getting Ahead

Be amusing: never tell unkind stories; above all, never tell long ones.

— BENJAMIN DISRAELI
British prime minister

Truths

Considering how dangerous everything is, nothing is really very frightening.

—GERTRUDE STEIN
Writer

Facing Life Head-On

If I had a formula for bypassing trouble, I would not pass it round. Trouble creates a capacity to handle it. I don't embrace trouble; that's as bad as treating it as an enemy. But I do say, meet it as a friend, for you'll see a lot of it and had better be on speaking terms with it.

—OLIVER WENDELL HOLMES
Jurist

Faith

In the depth of winter, I finally learned that within me lay an invincible summer.

—ALBERT CAMUS
Writer

Rules to Live By

Don't tell your problems
to people: eighty percent
don't care, and the other
twenty percent are glad
you have them.

—Lou Holtz
Football coach

What Really Matters

Life's meaning has always eluded me and I guess it always will. But I love it just the same.

—E. B. WHITE
Writer

Coping

Stress is an ignorant state. It believes that everything is an emergency. Nothing is that important. Just lie down.

—NATALIE GOLDBERG
Writer

Try, Try Again

I have not failed. I've just found 10,000 ways that won't work.

—THOMAS ALVA EDISON
Inventor

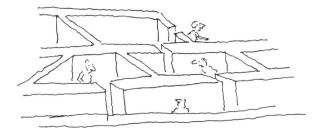

The Right Attitude

The important thing is not what they think of me, but what I think of them.

— VICTORIA
Queen of England

An Ironic Twist

I prefer to think that God is not dead, just drunk.

—JOHN HUSTON
Film director

Never Give Up

Never give in, never give in, never, never, never, never—in nothing, great or small, large or petty. Never give in except to convictions of honor and good sense.

— WINSTON CHURCHILL
British prime minister

Friends

We have fewer friends than we imagine, but more than we know.

—HUGO VON HOFMANNSTHAL
Writer

Perseverance

Strength comes from waiting.

—JOSÉ MARTÍ
Writer and Political activist

Things I've Learned

The average man doesn't wish to be told that it is a bull or a bear market. What he desires is to be told specifically which particular stock to buy or sell. He wants to get something for nothing. He does not wish to work. He doesn't even wish to have to think.

—JESSE LIVERMORE
Financier

Living on Less

I try to teach my heart to want nothing it can't have.

—ALICE WALKER
Writer

Balance

The world is so constructed, that if you wish to enjoy its pleasures, you must also endure its pains. Whether you like it or not, you cannot have one without the other.

—SWAMI BRAHMANANDA
Spiritual leader and Philosopher

What Really Matters

If people concentrated on the really important things in life, there'd be a shortage of fishing poles.

— DOUG LARSON
Writer

Rules to Live By

Forget past mistakes. Forget failures. Forget everything except what you're going to do now and do it.

—WILL DURANT
Historian

Self-Worth

I had to fight hard against loneliness, abuse, and the knowledge that any mistake I made would be magnified because I was the only black man out there. Many people resented my impatience and honesty, but I never cared about acceptance as much as I cared about respect.

—JACKIE ROBINSON
Baseball player

Survival Tactics

One can survive
everything nowadays,
except death, and live
down anything, except
a good reputation.

— OSCAR WILDE
Writer

The Silver Lining

The worse a situation becomes, the less it takes to turn it around—and the bigger the upside.

—GEORGE SOROS
Financier

Fighting Back

When your opponent's sittin' there holdin' all the aces, there's only one thing to do: Kick over the table.

—DEAN MARTIN
Actor and Singer

Taking Action

When in doubt, do something.

—HARRY CHAPIN
Musician

Rules to Live By

Never invest your money in anything that eats or needs repainting.

—BILLY ROSE
Theater producer

Acceptance

Teach us to care and not to care. Teach us to sit still.

—T. S. ELIOT
Writer

The Fine Art of Being Happy

The happiest people seem to be those who have no particular reason for being happy except that they are so.

— W. R. INGE
Clergyman and Writer

Try, Try Again

Never quit. It is the easiest cop-out in the world. Set a goal and don't quit until you attain it. When you do attain it, set another goal, and don't quit until you reach it. Never quit.

—BEAR BRYANT
Football coach

Money

Poverty of course is no disgrace, but it is damned annoying.

—WILLIAM PITT THE YOUNGER
British prime minister

True Grit

Courage and cheerfulness will not only carry you over the rough places in life, but will enable you to bring comfort and help to the weak-hearted and will console you in the sad hours.

—WILLIAM OSLER
Physician

It's How You Look at Things

A rich man is nothing but a poor man with money.

—W. C. FIELDS
Actor and Comedian

How to Live

You should examine
yourself daily. If you find
faults, you should correct
them. When you find none,
you should try even harder.

—XI ZHI
Philosopher

Taking Action

Dream! Dream! And then go for it!

—DESMOND TUTU
Cleric and Activist

Problems, Problems

A solved problem creates two new problems, and the best prescription for happy living is not to solve any more problems than you have to.

—RUSSELL BAKER
Columnist

Success and Failure

I've missed more than 9,000 shots in my career. I've lost almost 300 games; 26 times, I've been trusted to take the game-winning shot and missed. I've failed over and over and over again in my life. And that is why I succeed.

—MICHAEL JORDAN
Basketball player

The Silver Lining

Sweet are the uses of
 adversity;
Which, like the toad,
 ugly and venomous,
Wears yet a precious
 jewel in his head . . .

—WILLIAM SHAKESPEARE
Writer

An Ironic Twist

If it wasn't for bad luck, I wouldn't have no luck at all.

—ALBERT KING
Musician

Secrets of Getting Ahead

It is not enough to conquer; one must know how to seduce.

—François-Marie
Arouet Voltaire
Philosopher and Writer

Truths

There are two great rules of life, the one general and the other particular. The first is that everyone can, in the end, get what he wants if he only tries. This is the general rule. The particular rule is that every individual is more or less an exception to the general rule.

—SAMUEL BUTLER
Writer

Facing Life Head-On

Life only demands from you the strength you possess. Only one feat is possible—not to have run away.

—DAG HAMMARSKJÖLD
Diplomat

Hope

Hope can neither be affirmed nor denied. Hope is like a path in the countryside: Originally there was no path—yet, as people are walking all the time in the same spot, a way appears.

—LU XUN
Writer

Rules to Live By

Be aware of "yes" men. Generally, they are losers.

—BEAR BRYANT
Football coach

Counting Your Blessings

The hardest arithmetic to master is that which enables us to count our blessings.

—ERIC HOFFER
Social commentator

Success and Failure

Success makes life easier. It doesn't make living easier.

— BRUCE SPRINGSTEEN
Musician

Try, Try Again

If a man loses anything and goes back and looks carefully for it, he will find it.

—SITTING BULL
Lakota Sioux chief and Medicine man

The Right Attitude

If you can accept losing you can't win. If you can walk you can run. No one is ever hurt. Hurt is in your mind.

—VINCE LOMBARDI
American football coach

Testing Yourself

Any road followed precisely to its end leads precisely nowhere. Climb the mountain just a little bit to test it's a mountain. From the top of the mountain, you cannot see the mountain.

— FRANK HERBERT
Writer

Friends

It's the friends you can call
up at 4:00 A.M. who matter.

— MARLENE DIETRICH
Actress

Life Goes On

In life, unlike chess,
the game continues after
checkmate.

— ISAAC ASIMOV
Writer

Money

The trouble with the profit system has always been that it was highly unprofitable to most people.

—E.B. WHITE
Writer

Coping

Noble deeds and hot baths are the best cures for depression.

—DODIE SMITH
Writer

Living on Less

An object in possession
seldom retains the same
charm that it had in
pursuit.

—PLINY THE YOUNGER
Writer

Balance

An optimist is a person who sees a green light everywhere, while a pessimist sees only the red stoplight. . . . The truly wise person is colorblind.

> —ALBERT SCHWEITZER
> *Humanitarian and Philosopher*

Grace Under Pressure

It is dangerous to abandon one's self to the luxury of grief; it deprives one of courage, and even of the wish for recovery.

—HENRI FRÉDÉRIC AMIEL
Writer

We All Make Mistakes

I want to explain my
mistakes. This means
I do only the things I
completely understand.

—WARREN BUFFETT
Investor

True Grit

The greatest weakness of all weaknesses is to fear too much to appear weak.

—JACQUES-BÉNIGNE BOSSUET
Bishop and Theologian

Survival Tactics

It is not the strongest of the species that survives, nor the most intelligent that survives. It is the one that is the most adaptable to change.

—Charles Darwin
Naturalist

The Silver Lining

Only a man who knows what it is like to be defeated can reach down to the bottom of his soul and come up with the extra ounce of power it takes to win when the match is even.

—MUHAMMAD ALI
Boxer

Things I've Learned

If you haven't found something strange during the day, it hasn't been much of a day.

—J. A. WHEELER
Physicist

Taking Action

At the day of judgment we shall not be asked what we have read but what we have done.

—THOMAS À KEMPIS
Mystic

Secrets of Getting Ahead

If you want to catch more fish, use more hooks.

—GEORGE ALLEN
American football coach

Don't Worry, Be Happy

Every time is a time for comedy in a world of tension that would languish without it. But I cannot confine myself to lightness in a period of human life that demands light. . . . We all know that, as the old adage has it, "It is later than you think". . ., but I also say occasionally: "It is lighter than you think." In this light let's not look back in anger, or forward in fear, but around in awareness.

—James Thurber
Humorist and Cartoonist

Acceptance

Don't grieve. Anything you lose comes round in another form.

—RUMI (JALAL AD-DIN)
Poet and Mystic

An Ironic Twist

If you hear that someone is speaking ill of you, instead of trying to defend yourself you should say: "He obviously does not know me very well, since there are so many other faults he could have mentioned."

— EPICTETUS
Philosopher

Never Give Up

They could not capture me except under a white flag. They cannot hold me except with a chain.

—OSCEOLA
Seminole chief

True Grit

Plunge into the deep without fear, with the gladness of April in your heart.

—RABINDRANATH TAGORE
Writer and Philosopher

It's How You Look at Things

What comfort can the vortices of Descartes give to a man who has whirlwinds in his bowels?

— BENJAMIN FRANKLIN
Statesman

How to Live

Be gentle to all and stern with yourself.

— TERESA OF AVILA
Mystic and Nun

Taking Action

I leave this rule for others when I'm dead, be always sure you're right—then go ahead.

—DAVY CROCKETT
Soldier and Politician

Problems, Problems

We can't solve problems by using the same kind of thinking we used when we created them.

—ALBERT EINSTEIN
Physicist

Success and Failure

Q. How do you define success?

Writer MADELINE L'ENGLE:

A. If I have enough laughter, if I go to bed contented with myself and my life. I don't think the world's standards of success are that valid.

The Silver Lining

Mishaps are like knives that either serve us or cut us, as we grasp them by the blade or the handle.

— JAMES RUSSELL LOWELL
Poet, Editor, and Diplomat

You Might As Well Laugh

When we win, I'm so happy, I eat a lot. When we lose, I'm so depressed, I eat a lot. When we're rained out, I'm so disappointed, I eat a lot.

— TOMMY LASORDA
Baseball manager

Secrets of Getting Ahead

Put your heart, mind, intellect, and soul even to your smallest acts. This is the secret of success.

—SIVANANDA SARASWATI
Spiritual leader

Truths

The truth does not change according to our ability to stomach it.

—FLANNERY O'CONNOR
Writer

Facing Life Head-On

These are the times that try men's souls. The summer soldier and the sunshine patriot will, in this crisis, shrink from the service of their country; but he that stands it now, deserves the love and thanks of man and woman. Tyranny, like hell, is not easily conquered; yet we have this consolation with us, that the harder the conflict, the more glorious the triumph. What we obtain too

cheap, we esteem too lightly;
it is dearness only that gives
everything its value. I love the
man that can smile in trouble,
that can gather strength from
distress and grow brave by
reflection. 'Tis the business
of little minds to shrink; but
he whose heart is firm, and
whose conscience approves
his conduct, will pursue his
principles unto death.

— THOMAS PAINE
American revolutionary

Faith

When I despair, I remember
that all through history the way
of truth and love has always
won. There have been tyrants
and murderers and for a time
they seem invincible, but in the
end, they always fall
. . . think of it,
always.

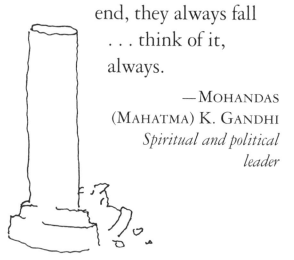

—MOHANDAS
(MAHATMA) K. GANDHI
*Spiritual and political
leader*

Rules to Live By

Always do sober
what you said you'd
do drunk. That will
teach you to keep
your mouth shut.

—ERNEST HEMINGWAY
Writer

What Really Matters

What's the subject of life—to get rich? All of those fellows out there getting rich could be dancing around the real subject of life.

—PAUL VOLCKER
Economist

Coping

Sometimes you just have to pee in the sink.

—CHARLES BUKOWSKI
Writer

Try, Try Again

It's never too late—in fiction or in life—to revise.

—NANCY THAYER
Writer

The Right Attitude

If I regarded my life from the point of view of the pessimist, I should be undone. I should seek in vain for the light that does not visit my eyes and the music that does not ring in my ears. I should beg night and day and never be satisfied. I should sit apart in awful solitude, a prey to fear and despair. But since I consider it a duty to myself and to others to be happy, I escape a misery worse than any physical deprivation.

—HELEN KELLER
Writer and Activist

Eat, Drink, and Be Merry

Wine: a constant proof that God loves us, and loves to see us happy. Wine makes daily living easier, less hurried, with fewer tensions and more tolerance.

—BENJAMIN FRANKLIN
Statesman

Testing Yourself

You never know how
a horse will pull until
you hook him to a
heavy load.

—BEAR BRYANT
Football coach

Friends
I have
seen that
in any great
undertaking it is
not enough for a man
to depend simply upon
himself.

—LONE MAN (ISNA-LA-WICA)
Teton Sioux warrior

Money

I am indeed rich, since my income is superior to my expense, and my expense is equal to my wishes.

—EDWARD GIBBON
Historian

Perseverance

Some people think that as soon as you plant a tree, it must bear fruit. We must allow it to grow a bit.

—Tunku Abdul Rahman Putra
Politician

Things I've Learned

I have seen wicked men and fools, a great many of both; and I believe they both get paid in the end; but the fools first.

—ROBERT LOUIS STEVENSON
Writer

Living on Less

Possessions, outward success, publicity, luxury—to me, these have always been contemptible. I believe that a simple and unassuming manner of life is best for everyone, best both for the body and the mind.

— ALBERT EINSTEIN
Physicist

Self-Worth

You say you are a
nameless man.
You are not to your wife
and to your child. You
will not long remain
so to your immediate
colleagues if you can
answer their simple
questions when they
come into your office.
You are not nameless
to me. Do not remain

nameless to yourself—
it is too sad a way to
be. Know your place in
the world and evaluate
yourself fairly, not in
terms of the naïve ideals
of your own youth, nor
in terms of what you
erroneously imagine your
teacher's ideals are.

—RICHARD FEYNMAN
Physicist,
in a letter to a colleague

Grace Under Pressure

It is foolish to tear
one's hair in grief,
as though sorrow
would be made less
by baldness.

— Marcus Tullius Cicero
Statesman

We All Make Mistakes

Nowadays most people die of a sort of creeping common sense, and discover when it is too late that the only things one never regrets are one's mistakes.

—OSCAR WILDE
Writer

Survival Tactics

Some of us think holding on makes us strong; but sometimes it is letting go.

—Hermann Hesse
Writer

The Silver Lining

When there is blood on the street, I am buying.

—Nathaniel Mayer
Victor Rothschild,
3rd Baron Rothschild
Banker

Hope

Don't part with your illusions. When they are gone you may still exist but you have ceased to live.

—MARK TWAIN
Writer

How to Live

We are what we pretend to be, so we must be careful about what we pretend to be.

—KURT VONNEGUT JR.
Writer

Don't Worry, Be Happy

Not a shred of evidence exists in favor of the idea that life is serious.

—BRENDAN GILL
Writer

Acceptance

I assumed that everything would lead to complete failure, but I decided that didn't matter—that would be my life.

—JASPER JOHNS JR.
Painter

The Fine Art of Being Happy

If we only wanted to be happy, it would be easy; but we want to be happier than other people, and that is almost always difficult, since we think them happier than they are.

—CHARLES DE SECONDAT,
BARON DE MONTESQUIEU
Philosopher

Never Give Up

It's not whether you get knocked down, it's whether you get up.

—VINCE LOMBARDI
American football coach

Money

Money is not the most important thing in the world. Love is. Fortunately, I love money.

—JACKIE MASON
Comedian

True Grit

The only real prison is fear, and the only real freedom is freedom from fear.

—AUNG SAN SUU KYI
Political activist

The Right Attitude

Failure is impossible.

—SUSAN B. ANTHONY
Suffragist

How to Live

Cling tooth and nail to the following rule: Not to give in to adversity, never to trust prosperity, and always to take full note of fortune's habit of behaving just as she pleases, treating her as if she were actually going to do everything it is in her power to do. Whatever you have been expecting for some time comes as less of a shock.

— LUCIUS ANNAEUS SENECA
Philosopher

Taking Action

Never confuse movement with action.

—ERNEST HEMINGWAY
Writer

Problems, Problems

Some problems are so complex that you have to be highly intelligent and well informed just to be undecided about them.

—LAURENCE J. PETER
Writer

Success and Failure

Lose as if you like it; win as if you were used to it.

—TOMMY HITCHCOCK
Polo player

The Silver Lining

Truly, it is in darkness that one finds the light, so when we are in sorrow, then this light is nearest of all to us.

— MEISTER ECKHART
(ECKHART VON HOCHHEIM)
Mystic

You Might As Well Laugh

More than any other time in history, mankind faces a crossroads. One path leads to despair and utter hopelessness. The other, to total extinction. Let us pray we have the wisdom to choose correctly.

— WOODY ALLEN
Film director

Secrets of Getting Ahead

To succeed in the world, it is much more necessary to possess the penetration to discover who is a fool than to discover who is a clever man.

—CATO THE ELDER
Statesman

Truths

Reality is that which, when you stop believing in it, doesn't go away.

— PHILIP K. DICK
Writer

Facing Life Head-On

We must embrace pain and burn it as fuel for our journey.

— KENJI MIYAZAWA
Writer

Hope

Hope is not the conviction that something will turn out well but the certainty that something makes sense, regardless of how it turns out.

—VÁCLAV HAVEL
Writer and Statesman

Rules to Live By

You cannot beat a roulette table unless you steal money from it.

—ALBERT EINSTEIN
Physicist

Counting Your Blessings

No matter how bad things are, they can always be worse. So what if my stroke left me with a speech impediment? Moses had one, and he did all right.

—KIRK DOUGLAS
Actor

Coping

Nothing happens to any man that he is not formed by nature to bear.

—MARCUS AURELIUS
Roman emperor and Philosopher

Try, Try Again

There is an old motto that runs, "If at first you don't succeed, try, try again." This is nonsense. It ought to read, "If at first you don't succeed, quit, quit at once."

—STEPHEN LEACOCK
Writer and Economist

The Right Attitude

My center is giving way, my right is in retreat; situation excellent. I shall attack!

—FERDINAND FOCH
French Marshal and Military theorist

Testing Yourself

It is not the critic who counts: not the man who points out how the strong man stumbles or where the doer of deeds could have done better. The credit belongs to the man who is actually in the arena, whose face is marred by dust and sweat and blood, who strives valiantly, who errs and comes up short again and again, because there is no effort without error or shortcoming, but who knows the great enthusiasms, the great devotions, who spends himself for a worthy cause; who, at the best, knows, in the end, the triumph of high achievement, and who, at the worst, if he fails, at least he fails while daring greatly, so that his place shall never be with those cold and timid souls who knew neither victory nor defeat.

—THEODORE ROOSEVELT
U.S. President

Eat, Drink, and Be Merry

When I hear music, I fear no danger. I am invulnerable. I see no foe. I am related to the earliest times, and to the latest.

—HENRY DAVID THOREAU
Writer

Friends

If you want to know who your friends are, get yourself a jail sentence.

—CHARLES BUKOWSKI
Writer

Money

Anyone who lives within their means suffers from a lack of imagination.

—OSCAR WILDE
Writer

Life Goes On

The pain passes, but the beauty remains.

—PIERRE-AUGUSTE RENOIR
Artist

Things I've Learned

What uses up a life is not so much its great tragedies as its small annoyances and the recurrent waste of time. It is not our enemies who wear us down, but rather our friends, or those half-friends who keep on wanting to meet us, although we have no corresponding desire to meet them.

—HENRY DE MONTHERLANT
Writer

Living on Less

Give me the luxuries in life and I will willingly do without the necessities.

—FRANK LLOYD WRIGHT
Architect

Balance

To gain that which is worth having, it may be necessary to lose everything else.

—BERNADETTE DEVLIN
Politician and Activist

Coping

Keep cool: it will all be one a hundred years hence.

—RALPH WALDO EMERSON
Essayist and Philosopher

We All Make Mistakes

All the mistakes I ever made were when I wanted to say "No" and said "Yes."

—Moss Hart
Playwright

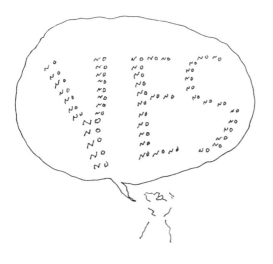

Self-Worth

Each man is good
in his sight. It is not
necessary for eagles
to be crows.

—SITTING BULL
Lakota Sioux chief

Survival Tactics

The human body has an enormous capacity for adjusting to trying circumstances. I have found that one can bear the unbearable if one can keep one's spirits strong even when one's body is being tested. Strong convictions are the secret of surviving deprivation; your spirit can be full even when your stomach is empty.

—NELSON MANDELA
Activist and South African President

The Silver Lining

Grief is itself a medicine.

— WILLIAM COWPER
Poet and Hymnodist

Life Goes On

It is the peculiar nature of the world to go on spinning no matter what sort of heartbreak is happening.

—SUE MONK KIDD
Writer

Taking Action

If you would be a reader,
read; if a writer, write.

— EPICTETUS
Philosopher

Rules to Live By

Never memorize what you
can look up in books.

— ALBERT EINSTEIN
Physicist

Acceptance

There is no security in your mansions or your fortresses, your family vaults or your banks or your double beds. Understand this fact, and you will be free. Accept it and you will be happy.

—CHRISTOPHER ISHERWOOD
Writer

The Fine Art of Being Happy

The trick is not how much pain you feel— but how much joy you feel. Any idiot can feel pain. Life is full of excuses to feel pain, excuses not to live, excuses, excuses, excuses.

—ERICA JONG
Writer

Never Give Up

Never confuse a single defeat with a final defeat.

—F. Scott Fitzgerald
Writer

Money

What's money? A man is a success if he gets up in the morning and gets to bed at night, and in between he does what he wants to.

—BOB DYLAN
Musician

True Grit

Courage is not simply one of the virtues but the form of every virtue at the testing point.

—C. S. LEWIS
Writer

It's How You Look at Things

When one door closes another door opens; but we so often look so long and so regretfully upon the closed door, that we do not see the ones which open for us.

— ALEXANDER GRAHAM BELL
Inventor

How to Live

Boldness, and again boldness, and always boldness!

—GEORGES-JACQUES DANTON
Revolutionary

Taking Action

Often the difference between a successful person and a failure is not one's better abilities or ideas, but the courage that one has to bet on one's ideas, to take a calculated risk—and to act.

— ANDRÉ MALRAUX
Writer

Life's Lessons

The thing that's important to know is that you never know. You're always sort of feeling your way.

—DIANE ARBUS
Photographer

Success and Failure

You know what makes a good loser? Practice.

—ERNEST HEMINGWAY
Writer

The Silver Lining

I don't like people who have never fallen or stumbled. Their virtue is lifeless and it isn't of much value. Life hasn't revealed its beauty to them.

—BORIS PASTERNAK
Writer

Secrets of Getting Ahead

Keep your eyes open and your mouth shut.

—JOHN STEINBECK
Writer

Truths

How many legs does a dog have if you call the tail a leg? Four. Calling a tail a leg doesn't make it a leg.

— Abraham Lincoln
U.S. President

Facing Life Head-On

In difficult and hopeless
situations the boldest plans
are the safest.

— TITUS LIVY
Historian

Faith

If you have abandoned one faith, do not abandon all faith. There is always an alternative to the faith we lose. Or is it the same faith under another mask?

—GRAHAM GREENE
Writer

Rules to Live By

When you want to fool the world, tell the truth.

—OTTO VON BISMARCK
German chancellor

Things I've Learned

The oldest, shortest words —"yes" and "no"— are those which require the most thought.

— PYTHAGORAS
Philosopher

Coping

Without my morning coffee I'm just like a dried-up piece of roast goat.

—JOHANN SEBASTIAN BACH
Composer

Try, Try Again

Big shots are only little shots who keep shooting.

—CHRISTOPHER MORLEY
Journalist and Writer

The Right Attitude

We didn't lose the game; we just ran out of time.

—VINCE LOMBARDI
American football coach

Eat, Drink, and Be Merry

He who does not like wine, song, and wife, Remains a fool for the whole of his life.

— MARTIN LUTHER
Theologian

Testing Yourself

When heaven is about to confer a great responsibility on any man, it will exercise his mind with suffering, subject his sinews and bones to hard work, expose his body to hunger, put him to poverty, place obstacles in the paths of his deeds, so as to stimulate his mind, harden his nature, and improve wherever he is incompetent.

—MENG-TZU
Philosopher

Friends

Lots of people want to ride with you in the limo, but what you want is someone who will take the bus with you when the limo breaks down.

—OPRAH WINFREY
Television host and Philanthropist

Money

I must say I hate money, but it's the lack of it that I hate most.

—KATHERINE MANSFIELD
Writer

Perseverance

First they ignore you,
then they laugh at you,
then they fight you,
then you win.

— MOHANDAS (MAHATMA) K.
GANDHI
Spiritual and political leader

Counting Your Blessings

I have been walking onto ball fields for sixteen years, and I've never received anything but kindness and encouragement from you fans. I have had the great honor to have played with these great veteran ballplayers on my left—Murderers Row, our championship team of 1927. I have had the further honor living and playing with these men on my right—the Bronx Bombers, the Yankees of today. I have been given fame and undeserved praise by the boys up there behind the wire, my friends, the sports writers. I have worked under the two greatest managers of all time, Miller Huggins and Joe McCarthy. I have a mother and father who fought to give me health and a solid background in my youth. I have a wife, a companion for life, who has shown me more courage than I ever knew. People all say that I've had a bad break. But today—today I consider myself the luckiest man on the face of the earth.

—LOU GEHRIG
Baseball player,
in his "Farewell to Baseball
Address" at Yankee Stadium

Things I've Learned

I long ago came to the conclusion that all life is six to five against.

— DAMON RUNYON
Writer

Living on Less

If you have a garden and a library, you have everything you need.

— MARCUS TULLIUS CICERO
Statesman

Balance

I f we had no
winter, the spring
would not be so
pleasant; if we did
not sometimes
taste of adversity,
prosperity would not
be so welcome.

—ANNE DUDLEY BRADSTREET
Poet

Grace Under Pressure

You can overcome anything if you don't bellyache.

—BERNARD BARUCH
Financier

We All Make Mistakes

To swear off making mistakes is very easy. All you have to do is swear off having ideas.

—LEO BURNETT
Advertising executive

True Grit

Bravery is the capacity to perform properly even when scared half to death.

—OMAR BRADLEY
U.S. general

Survival Tactics

One of the most difficult things everyone has to learn is that for your entire life you must keep fighting and adjusting if you hope to survive. No matter who you are or what your position is you must keep fighting for whatever it is you desire to achieve.

—GEORGE ALLEN
American football coach

The Silver Lining

It is by going down into the abyss that we recover the treasures of life. Where you stumble, there lies your treasure.

— JOSEPH CAMPBELL
Writer

Money

I cannot afford to waste my time making money.

—JEAN LOUIS AGASSIZ
Zoologist and Geologist

Taking Action

Go! Go! Go! It makes no difference where, just so you go! go! go! Remember at the first opportunity: Go!

—JEANETTE RANKIN
*First female representative
in U.S. Congress*

How to Live

Live like a mud-fish:
its skin is bright and
shiny even though it
lives in mud.

— RAMAKRISHNA
Mystic

Don't Worry, Be Happy

Nothing is miserable unless you think it is so.

—BOETHIUS
Statesman and Philosopher

Acceptance

Child, the key is to love your wounds.

—SARAH "SADIE" DELANY
Writer and Civil Rights activist

The Fine Art of Being Happy

We should all do what, in the long run, gives us joy, even if it is only picking grapes or sorting the laundry.

— E.B. WHITE
Writer

Never Give Up

People of mediocre ability sometimes achieve outstanding success because they don't know when to quit. Most men succeed because they are determined to.

—GEORGE ALLEN
American football coach

Money

Is it not sheer madness to live poor to die rich?

—JUVENAL
Writer

True Grit

People who think of retreating before a battle has been fought ought to have stayed home.

—MICHEL NEY, DUC D'ELCHINGEN
French marshal

The Right Attitude

We are all in the gutter, but some of us are looking at the stars.

—OSCAR WILDE
Writer

How to Live

Finish each day and be done with it. You have done what you could. Some blunders and absurdities no doubt crept in; forget them as soon as you can. Tomorrow is a new day; you shall begin it well and serenely.

—RALPH WALDO EMERSON
Essayist and Philosopher

Taking Action

You miss 100 percent of
the shots you never take.

—WAYNE GRETZKY
Hockey player

Problems, Problems

A problem is a chance for
you to do your best.

—DUKE ELLINGTON
Musician

Success and Failure

Success is going from failure to failure without a loss of enthusiasm.

— WINSTON CHURCHILL
British prime minister

The Silver Lining

Adversity not only draws people together but brings forth that beautiful inward friendship, just as the cold winter forms ice-figures on the window panes which the warmth of the sun effaces.

—SØREN KIERKEGAARD
Philosopher

Tongue in Cheek

Just when things look darkest, they go black.

—PAUL NEWMAN
Actor

Secrets of Getting Ahead

You can become a winner only if you are willing to walk over the edge.

—DAMON RUNYON
Writer

Truths

Life would be tragic if it weren't funny.

—STEPHEN HAWKING
Physicist

Facing Life Head-On

I must not fear. Fear is the mind-killer. Fear is the little-death that brings total obliteration. I will face my fear. I will permit it to pass over me and through me. And when it has gone past I will turn the inner eye to see its path. Where the fear has gone there will be nothing. Only I will remain.

—FRANK HERBERT
Writer

Hope

I am a little deaf, a little blind, a little impotent, and on top of this are two or three abominable infirmities, but nothing destroys my hope.

—FRANÇOIS-MARIE
AROUET VOLTAIRE
Philosopher and Writer

Counting Your Blessings

Every day is a gift—even if it sucks.

—SHERRY HOCHMAN
Writer

Coping

When I get sick of what men do, I have only to walk a few steps in another direction to see what spiders do. Or what the weather does. This sustains me very well indeed.

—E.B. WHITE
Writer

Try, Try Again

If at first you succeed,
quit trying.

—WARREN BUFFETT
Investor

The Right Attitude

Pessimism never won any
battle.

—DWIGHT D. EISENHOWER
U.S. General and President

You Might As Well Laugh

The glass is always half empty. And cracked. And I just cut my lip on it. And chipped a tooth.

— JANEANE GAROFALO
Comedian

Testing Yourself

Man's greatest actions are performed in minor struggles. Life, misfortune, isolation, abandonment and poverty are battlefields which have their heroes—obscure heroes who are at times greater than illustrious heroes.

— Victor Hugo
Writer

Friends

Prosperity makes friends, adversity tries them.

— PUBLILIUS SYRUS
Writer

Money

Money will not make you happy, and happy will not make you money.

— GROUCHO MARX
Comedian

Perseverance

If there is no dull and determined effort, there will be no brilliant achievement.

— HSÜN-TZU
Philosopher

What Really Matters

When I get a little money,
I buy books; if any is left,
I buy food and clothes.

— DESIDERIUS ERASMUS
Humanist and Scholar

Living on Less

To be without some of
the things you want
is an indispensable part of
happiness.

—BERTRAND RUSSELL
Philosopher

Truths

Nobody gets justice. People only get good luck or bad luck.

—ORSON WELLES
Film director

Grace Under Pressure

I have no need of your God-damned sympathy. I wish only to be entertained by some of your grosser reminiscences.

— ALEXANDER WOOLLCOTT
Critic,
to someone who sent him a
get-well note when he was sick

Things I've Learned

I am discounting reports of UFOs. Why would they appear only to cranks and weirdos?

—STEPHEN HAWKING
Physicist

Self-Worth

I am more important than my problems.

—JOSÉ FERRER
Actor

Survival Tactics

To survive it is often necessary to fight and to fight you have to dirty yourself.

—GEORGE ORWELL
Writer

The Silver Lining

There is no education like adversity.

—BENJAMIN DISRAELI
British prime minister

Fighting Back

When you see a rattlesnake poised to strike, you do not wait until he has struck before you crush him.

—FRANKLIN D. ROOSEVELT
U.S. President

Taking Action

If you keep thinking about what you want to do or what you hope will happen, you don't do it, and it won't happen.

—DESIDERIUS ERASMUS
Humanist and Scholar

How to Live

Always do right. This will gratify some people and astonish the rest.

— MARK TWAIN
Writer

Don't Worry, Be Happy

What are you laughing at?
The joke's on you.

—HORACE
Poet

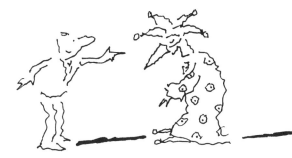

Taking Action

The great French Marshal Lyautey once asked his gardener to plant a tree. The gardener objected that the tree was slow growing and would not reach maturity for a hundred years. The Marshal replied, "In that case, there is no time to lose; plant it this afternoon!"

— JOHN F. KENNEDY
U.S. President

The Fine Art of Being Happy

If you want to be happy, be.

—LEO TOLSTOY
Writer

Never Give Up

Don't think of retiring from the world until the world will be sorry that you retire. I hate a fellow whom pride or cowardice or laziness drives into a corner, and who does nothing when he is there but sit and growl. Let him come out as I do, and bark.

—SAMUEL JOHNSON
Writer and Lexicographer

Money

If you owe your bank
a hundred pounds,
you have a problem.
But if you owe a
million, it has.

—JOHN MAYNARD KEYNES
Economist

True Grit

The difference between a brave man and a coward is a coward thinks twice before jumping in the cage with a lion. The brave man doesn't know what a lion is. He just thinks he does.

—CHARLES BUKOWSKI
Writer

It's How You Look at Things

Is not disease the rule of existence? There is not a lily pad floating on the river but has been riddled by insects. Almost every shrub and tree has its gall, oftentimes esteemed its chief ornament and scarcely to be distinguished from the fruit. If misery loves company, misery has company enough. Now, at midsummer, find me a perfect leaf or fruit.

— HENRY DAVID THOREAU
Writer

How to Live

Wanna fly, you got to give up the shit that weights you down.

— TONI MORRISON
Writer

Taking Action

S tart by doing the necessary, then the possible, and suddenly you are doing the impossible.

—FRANCIS OF ASSISI
Friar and Founder of religious order

Problems, Problems

No problem is too big to
run away from.

—CHARLES M. SCHULZ
Cartoonist

Success and Failure

The sun don't shine on the
same dog's ass all the time.

—JIM "CATFISH" HUNTER
Pitcher

The Silver Lining

Adversity makes men, and prosperity makes monsters.

—Victor Hugo
Writer

You Might As Well Laugh

If you can keep your head when all about you are losing theirs, it's just possible you haven't grasped the situation.

—JEAN KERR
Writer

Secrets of Getting Ahead

It ain't enough to get the breaks. You gotta know how to use 'em.

—HUEY P. LONG
Politician

Facing Life Head-On

In the face of danger, worms dig themselves into the earth. Men rise up and fight!

—LUIS MUÑOZ RIVERA
Journalist and Politician

Hope

Hope begins in the dark, the stubborn hope that if you just show up and try to do the right thing, the dawn will come. You wait and watch and work: You don't give up.

—ANNE LAMOTT
Writer

Rules to Live By

One of these days in your travels a guy is going to come up to you and show you a nice brand-new deck of cards on which the seal is not yet broken, and this guy is going to offer to bet you that he can make the jack of spades jump out of the deck and squirt cider in your ear. But, son, do not bet this man, for as sure as you stand there, you are going to wind up with an earful of cider.

—DAMON RUNYON
Writer

What Really Matters

We can do no great things—only small things with great love.

—MOTHER TERESA
Humanitarian

Try, Try Again

Whoever said anybody has a right to give up?

—MARIAN WRIGHT EDELMAN
Activist

Success and Failure

Flops are part of life's menu.

—ROSALIND RUSSELL
Actress

Testing Yourself

When we are no longer able to change a situation, we are challenged to change ourselves.

— VIKTOR FRANKL
Psychologist

Friends

If you don't have enemies, you don't have character.

—PAUL NEWMAN
Actor

How to Live

Don't ever become a pessimist . . . a pessimist is correct oftener than an optimist, but an optimist has more fun— and neither can stop the march of events.

—ROBERT A. HEINLEIN
Writer

Money

With enough insider information and a million dollars, you can go broke in a year.

— WARREN BUFFETT
Investor

Life Goes On

In three words I can sum up everything I've learned about life: It goes on.

—ROBERT FROST
Poet

Things I've Learned

There are some people that if they don't know, you can't tell 'em.

—LOUIS ARMSTRONG
Musician

Living on Less

There must be more to life than having everything.

—MAURICE SENDAK
Writer and Illustrator

We All Make Mistakes

Mistakes that are perceived as mistakes are often not mistakes at all.

— KIRK DOUGLAS
Actor

Grace Under Pressure

It's not what happens to you, but how you react to it that matters.

— EPICTETUS
Philosopher

Balance

S ome days you're a bug. Some days you're a windshield.

—PRICE COBB
Race car driver

Self-Worth

You've no idea what a poor
opinion I have of myself,
and how little I deserve it.

— WILLIAM GILBERT
Playwright and Librettist

Survival Tactics

If you're going through hell, keep going.

— WINSTON CHURCHILL
British prime minister

The Silver Lining

If ours is truly an apocalyptic time, it may promise a new beginning rather than an end. We could not go on living with stale ideas. Certainly, we are faced with an extreme psychological test. The way to pass it is to accept the idea that life has rebelled and plunged us into such uncertainty because we have too long humiliated it. A season of change does not necessarily mean the collapse of civilization.

— FEDERICO FELLINI
Film director

Truths

The only sure thing about luck is that it will change.

—BRET HARTE
Writer

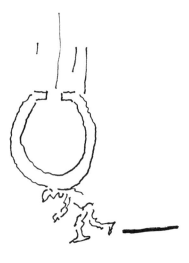

Fighting Back

I never quarrel, sir. But I sometimes fight, sir, and whenever I fight, sir, a funeral follows.

— THOMAS HART BENTON
Politician

How to Live

Mix a little foolishness
with your prudence:
It's good to be silly at
the right moment.

—Horace
Poet

Don't Worry, Be Happy

D o not anticipate
trouble, or
worry about what
may never happen.
Keep in the sunlight.

—BENJAMIN FRANKLIN
Statesman

Who's Quoted

Hank (Henry Louis) Aaron (1934–) American baseball player; Major League record holder for career home runs for 33 years until 2007; played with the Milwaukee and Atlanta Braves, and the Milwaukee Brewers; elected to National Baseball Hall of Fame in his first year of eligibility.

Jean Louis Agassiz (1807–73) Swiss-American zoologist and geologist; considered a founding father of the modern scientific tradition in America; although a renowned paleontologist, opposed Darwin's theory of evolution.

Muhammad Ali (1942–) American boxer; three-time world heavyweight boxing champion; renowned also for his quick-witted repartee.

Dante Alighieri (1265–1321) Florentine poet; author of the *Divina Commedia* (Divine Comedy), an allegorical poem of the poet's journey through Hell, Purgatory, and ultimately Paradise—considered one of the world's greatest works and a masterpiece of Italian literature.

George Allen (1918–90) American football coach; famed for innovative and inspirational coaching; third-best winning percentage in the NFL; led the Washington Redskins to the Super Bowl.

Woody Allen (*Alan Stewart Konigsberg*) (1935–)
American film director; writes and directs both serious
drama and screwball comedies, including *Annie Hall*,
winner of four Academy Awards, including Best
Picture.

Walter Alston (1911–84) American baseball player
and manager; led Brooklyn Dodgers to the World
Series pennant in 1955; won several more pennants
after the Dodgers moved to Los Angeles.

Henri-Frédéric Amiel (1821–81) Swiss philosopher
and critic; professor of philosophy at University of
Geneva; famous for his masterpiece of self-analysis
Journal Intime (Private Journal) published after his death.

Maya Angelou (1928–) American poet, memoirist,
and actress; best known for series of memoirs,
beginning with *I Know Why the Caged Bird Sings*.

Susan B. Anthony (1820–1906) American
suffragist, editor, and newspaper publisher; leader of
American women's suffrage movement; also involved
in temperance and abolitionist movements.

Thomas Aquinas (*Thomas of Aquin or Aquino*)
(ca. 1225–74) Italian philosopher and Dominican
monk; considered the preeminent Catholic scholastic
philosopher and theologian; combined Aristotelian
and Platonic thought with Christian theology; great
influence on later medieval and modern philosophy.

Diane Arbus (1923–71) American photographer; famous for documentary photographs, especially of subjects such as circus freaks, twins, and midgets; work marked by a stark style, irony, and psychological effect.

Aristophanes (450–ca. 385 B.C.) Greek playwright; greatest comic writer of Athenian democracy; known as the Father of Old Comedy; wrote during the Peloponnesian War satires, which skewered many contemporary figures, still admired today as masterpieces.

Lance Armstrong (1971–) American cyclist; winner of the Tour de France for a record-breaking seven consecutive years, from 1999 to 2005; cancer survivor and activist.

Louis Armstrong (1901–71) American jazz trumpeter and singer; called "Satchmo"; a jazz innovator and first major jazz virtuoso; appeared in more than fifty films and toured worldwide well into his later years.

Isaac Asimov (1920–92) American writer and scientist; famous for popularizing science and for general fiction, including groundbreaking science fiction, such as the novels of the *Foundation* series.

St. Augustine (*St. Aurelius Augustinus; St. Augustine of Hippo*) (354–430) North African religious leader/writer/ theologian; became bishop of Hippo; best known for his autobiographical *Confessions* and the twenty-two–book work, *The City of God*.

Marcus Aurelius Antoninus Augustus

(121–180) Roman emperor and philosopher; known as one of Rome's greatest Caesars; author of Stoic philosophy classic *The Meditations*.

Johann Sebastian Bach (1685–1750) German composer and organist; considered one of the greatest classical composers and a superb craftsman of Baroque music in virtually all genres; best known in his own lifetime as a master organist.

Russell Baker (1925–) American essayist and humourist; best known for his satirical "Observer" columns in *The New York Times*; winner of the Pulitzer Prize.

J. M. Barrie *(Sir James Matthew Barrie, 1st Baronet OM)* (1860–1937) Scottish novelist and playwright; creator of childhood classic *Peter Pan*.

John Barrymore *(John Sidney Blythe)* (1882–1942) American actor; famed for his Shakespearean roles, particularly Hamlet; often called the greatest actor of his generation.

Bernard Baruch (1870–1965) American financier, statesman, and presidential economic adviser; rose through the ranks from office boy to successful financier via speculation; purportedly withdrew his money from the stock market just before the crash in 1929.

Max Beerbohm (*Sir Henry Maximilian Beerbohm*) (1872–1956) American caricaturist and writer; his sophisticated drawings uniquely captured pretentiousness or absurdity of his famous contemporaries.

Alexander Graham Bell (1847–1922) American scientist and inventor; won first U.S. patent for the telephone; worked with hydrofoils and aeronautics; a founder of the National Geographic Society.

Thomas Hart Benton (1782–1858) American senator representing Missouri; nicknamed "Old Bullion" for his gold policies; a staunch upholder of Manifest Destiny or westward expansion; noted for his personal integrity.

Otto von Bismarck (*Otto Eduard Leopold von Bismarck, Count of Bismarck-Schönhausen, Duke of Lauenburg, Prince of Bismarck*) (1815–98) German chancellor; as Prussian minister helped engineer the Franco-Prussian War, which led to the creation of a united Germany; widely credited (along with Britain's Benjamin Disraeli) with maintaining peace in Europe during the late 1800s.

Boethius (*Anicius Manlius Severinus Boethius*) (ca. 480–ca. 524) Roman statesman and philosopher;

often called "the last of the Romans"; unjustly condemned for treachery; while in prison composed his most famous work *The Consolation of Philosophy*.

Jacques-Bénigne Bossuet (1627–1704) French bishop and theologian; court preacher to Louis XIV of France; renowned orator; one of the best stylists in French; a staunch advocate of royal absolutism.

Peg Bracken (1918–2007) American writer; best known for her humourous yet helpful books, such as *The I Hate to Cook Book*.

Malcolm Bradbury (1932–2000) American writer; prominent academic and expert on the modern novel; best known for his own novels, notably *The History Man*, a satire of academic life.

Omar Nelson Bradley (1893–1981) American soldier; commander of the 12th Army Group in the battle for Germany; later became first permanent chairman of Joint Chiefs of Staff; known as "the Soldier's General" because of his care of and compassion for troops under his command.

Anne Bradstreet (ca. 1612–72) American poet; known as America's first poet, or at least the first notable poet; the first woman to be published in colonial America; focused on domestic and religious themes.

Brahmananda (1863–1922) Hindu philosopher; disciple and transmitter of teachings of Sri Ramakrishna.

Mel Brooks (1926–) American director and writer; became the resident comic at New York's Catskill Mountain resort of Grossinger's; went on to produce acclaimed comedies, including classics *The Producers* and *Young Frankenstein*.

Paul William "Bear" Bryant (1913–83) American football coach; best known as coach of University of Alabama's "Crimson Tide" football team, leading it to several championships.

Warren Buffett (1930–) American investor and philanthropist; dubbed the "Oracle of Omaha" for his investment prowess; ranked the richest man in the world by *Forbes* magazine in 2008.

Charles Bukowski (1920–94) American writer; called the "Poet Laureate of Skid Row," for acclaimed writing on drinking, horse racing, and everyday life in a poor section of Los Angeles.

Robert Jones Burdette (1844–1914) American Baptist minister and humourist; wrote light columns in the Burlington (Iowa) *Hawk Eye*, which brought his homespun humour to national attention—and spawned national lecture tours.

Leo Burnett (1891–1971) American advertising executive; founded own agency in Chicago, now known as Leo Burnett Worldwide; creator of such advertising icons as Jolly Green Giant and Tony the Tiger.

Samuel Butler (1835–1902) English writer; best known for Utopian satire *Erehwon* and his anti-establishment *The Way of All Flesh*, which challenged Victorian-era conventions.

Joseph Campbell (1904–87) American mythologist, writer, and philosopher; best known for work in comparative mythology and as popularizer of world myths on television; famed for his advice to all strivers: "follow your bliss."

Albert Camus (1913–60) Algerian-born French writer; winner of Nobel Prize; considered a prominent existentialist writer (though he himself rejected the term); though fascinated by the seeming senselessness of life, he was devoted to opposing the philosophy of nihilism.

George Washington Carver (1864–1943) American agricultural scientist and educator; born into slavery, rose to become an eminent educator; advocated the now-accepted movement away from single-crop farming; showed how common crops such as peanuts could produce many common products.

Cato, the Elder (*Marcus Porcius*) (234–149 B.C.) Roman statesman; held most high offices in Rome; also known as Cato the Censor; famous for advocacy of both the old Roman virtues and the war against the rising power of Carthage.

Cervantes *(Miguel de Cervantes Saavedra)*
(1547–1616) Spanish writer; best known for novel,
Don Quixote; the comic adventures of a knight who
carries his notions of romance a bit too far, a classic
of Western literature, had great influence on the
Spanish language.

Harry Chapin (1942–1981) American musician;
folk rock singer and songwriter known for haunting
songs such as "Taxi" and "Cat's in the Cradle;" also
a humanitarian focusing on the fight against world
hunger who was awarded a posthumous Congressional
Gold Medal for his work; killed in an automobile
accident.

John Cheever (1912–82) American writer; Pulitzer
Prize–winning author of novels and short stories;
sometimes called the "Chekhov of the suburbs" for his
dark and ironic descriptions of the spiritual problems
and manners of middle-class American life.

Winston Churchill (1874–1965) English statesman;
member of Parliament who rose to British prime
minister; rallied the U.K. against Nazi Germany
during World War II; celebrated as one of the last of
the classic English orators.

Cicero *(Marcus Tullius Cicero)* (106–43 B.C.) Roman
orator, statesman, and writer; brilliant legal orator
who rose through the ranks of Roman government;
wrote many famous rhetorical and philosophical works;

eventually lost both popularity and power—and was killed by henchmen of his enemy Mark Antony.

Price Cobb (1954–) American race car driver; winner of the 1990 Le Mans; owned an Indy team; author of several auto-racing books.

Leonard Cohen (1934–) Canadian singer, songwriter, poet; noted for complex explorations of human loneliness and yearnings in his music; cited by Lou Reed as among the "highest and most influential echelon of songwriters" upon his election to the Rock and Roll Hall of Fame.

Calvin Coolidge (1872–1933) Thirtieth president of the U.S.; brought public confidence back to the White House after the scandals of the Harding years; a fiscal conservative who favoured limited government; known for his extreme taciturnity.

William Cowper (1731–1800) English poet and hymnodist; most famous for his bucolic poetry, which altered the direction of English poetry; collaborated with John Newton on the famous "Olney Hymns."

Crazy Horse (*Tashonka Yotanka*) (ca. 1842–77) Oglala Sioux chief; a principal leader of Sioux uprising, in which he led the Sioux in the Battle of Little Bighorn, defeating U.S. General George Custer; surrendered in 1877; was killed resisting imprisonment.

Davy Crockett (1786–1836) American frontiersman, soldier, politician, and folk hero known as "King of the Wild Frontier"; represented Tennessee in the U.S. House of Representatives; a hero of the Texas Revolution; died at the Battle of the Alamo.

Georges-Jacques Danton (1759–94) French jurist and one of the early leaders in the French Revolution; president of the new Republican Committee of Public Safety; served as a moderating influence; accused of excessive leniency during the Terror and was guillotined by radicals.

Clarence Seward Darrow (1857–1938) American lawyer; member of American Civil Liberties Union; best known for famous defense of John Scopes in the "Monkey Trial," in which he opposed statesman William Jennings Bryan and defended the teaching of evolution.

Charles Robert Darwin (1809–82) English naturalist; pioneering scientist who developed the theory of evolution, as propounded in *On the Origin of Species*.

Sarah Louise "Sadie" Delany (1889–1999) American teacher and writer; first African American to teach domestic science in New York; gained national fame after cowriting with her sister *Having Our Say: The Delany Sisters' First 100 Years*.

Bernadette Devlin (1947–) Irish politician; activist in Northern Ireland; became youngest member of the British House of Commons; founding member of Irish Republican Socialist party.

Philip K. Dick (1928–82) American science fiction writer; explored complex metaphysical and visionary themes; among his works are *Do Androids Dream of Electric Sheep?* (the basis for the sci-fi classic films *Blade Runner*) and *Total Recall*.

Marlene Dietrich (1901–92) German-born American actress and singer; top German star in the 1920s when cast by U.S. director Josef von Sternberg as Lola in *The Blue Angel*, which brought her international fame; became top Hollywood star.

Annie Dillard (1945–) American poet, essayist, and novelist; best known for narrative nonfiction, much of it autobiographical; winner of Pulitzer Prize in 1975.

Walt Disney (1901–66) American animator; entertainment entrepreneur; father of such icons as Mickey Mouse and Donald Duck; founder of the innovative Walt Disney empire.

Benjamin Disraeli (1804–81) British statesman and novelist; was member of Parliament and prime minister; averted war in Europe at Congress of Berlin in 1878; celebrated as a popular novelist, particularly for the romances *Sybil* and *Vivian Grey*.

J. P. Donleavy (1926–) Irish American writer; born in New York, but became an Irish citizen after World War II; best known for *The Ginger Man*, the racy adventures of a young American in Dublin.

Fyodor Dostoevsky (1821–81) Russian writer; novels, including *Crime and Punishment* and *The Brothers Karamazov*, explored psychological complexity in nineteenth-century Russia with a universalist theme; considered founder of modern existential novel.

Kirk Douglas (*Issur Danielovitch*) (1916–) American actor, director, writer; a top box-office draw beginning in the late '40s; portrayed vibrant, forceful characters through the 1980s; later became active in civic affairs; also wrote novels and two autobiographies.

Frederick Douglass (*Frederick Augustus Washington Bailey*) (1817–95) American abolitionist and writer; born a slave, he escaped, changed his name, and moved to Massachusetts where he worked for the abolitionist movement; known for his stirring and eloquent speeches; later worked as journalist; served as U.S. diplomat.

Will Durant (1885–1981) American historian and essayist; best known as a popularizer of history—and for his massive eleven-volume work, *The Story of Civilization* (written, in part, with his wife, Ariel), which covers civilization from prehistory to the nineteenth century.

Bob Dylan *(Robert Allen Zimmerman)* (1941–)
American musician, singer-songwriter, and artist;
rose to prominence in the 1960s with folk-rock hits
like *Blowin' in the Wind*; has remained a musical
innovator throughout his career.

Meister Eckhart *(Eckhart von Hochheim)*
(ca. 1260–ca. 1327) German Christian mystic and
theologian; a member of the Dominican order; known
for his teachings of mystical union with God.

Marion Wright Edelman (1939–) American
activist; children's rights advocate across a broad
range of issues, including child care, abuse,
homelessness, foster care, youth pregnancy
prevention; president and founder of the Children's
Defense Fund.

Thomas Alva Edison (1847–1931) American
inventor; credited with inventing the phonograph
and the long-lasting electric light bulb; his
pioneering research laboratory, which was among
the first to use teams of inventors and scientists,
produced 1,093 U.S. patents.

Albert Einstein (1879–1955) German-Swiss–
American mathematical physicist; one of the greatest
theoreticians in physics; formulated specific and
general theories of relativity; urged international
control of nuclear weapons.

Dwight D. Eisenhower (1890–1969) American president and soldier; as five-star U.S. general and Supreme Commander of the Allied forces in Europe, led troops to victory over Nazi Germany; as thirty-fourth U.S. president served from 1953 to 1961.

T. S. Eliot (1888–1965) Anglo-American poet, critic, and editor; first book of poems, *Prufrock and Other Observations*, established his reputation; *The Waste Land* considered by many the most influential poetic work of the twentieth century; awarded Nobel Prize for literature in 1948.

Duke Ellington (*Edward Kennedy Ellington*) (1899–1974) American pianist, composer, and bandleader; one of the leading jazz bandleaders, with longstanding engagement at Harlem nightspot, the Cotton Club; famous for such standards such as *Sophisticated Lady* and *Mood Indigo*.

Ralph Waldo Emerson (1803–82) American poet and essayist; leader of the American transcendentalist school; argued for spiritual independence, intuition, and individualism.

Epictetus (ca. 55–ca. 125) Greco-Roman philosopher; a former slave; one of the most influential Stoic philosophers; said that fate controls our lives and we must accept its vicissitudes calmly and dispassionately.

Desiderius Erasmus (ca. 1469–1536) Dutch theological scholar and humanist; a leader of the Northern Renaissance; translated and edited numerous classical Greek, Roman, and early Church authors; challenged old scholastic methods of biblical scholarship.

Federico Fellini (1920–93) Italian film director; began as a court reporter and cartoonist; broke into film with help from director Roberto Rossellini; directed numerous celebrated films, including *La Strada* and *Amacord*, garnering four Oscars in the process.

José Ferrer (1912–92) Puerto Rican–American director and actor, worked in film, in television, and on stage; best known for his portrayal of Cyrano de Bergerac on stage and in film; won Academy Award for the film version.

Richard P. Feynman (1918–88) American physicist; worked on the first atomic bomb, thereafter a professor at California Institute of Technology; a pioneer in quantum electrodynamics; won Nobel Prize in 1965; also well known for outspoken, humourous lecturing style and popular books.

W. C. Fields (1880–1946) American comedic actor, also known as the most successful comedy juggler of his generation; starred in numerous Hollywood comedies where his bulbous nose and irascible witticisms became personal trademarks and classics of modern comedy; films include *The Bank Dick* and *My Little Chickadee*.

F. Scott Fitzgerald (1896–1940) American writer; one of the leading chroniclers of the Jazz Age of the 1920s, in works such as *The Great Gatsby*.

Ferdinand Foch (1851–1929) French military leader; credited with stopping the German advance into France during World War I; as Supreme Commander of the Allied Armies, led Allies to victory and an armistice with Germany; also distinguished as military thinker and strategist.

Francis of Assisi (1182–1226) Italian religious leader and saint; born to a rich merchant's family; became a friar and founder of Order of Mendicant Friars or Franciscans, who take a vow of poverty and obedience; patron saint of animals and ecology.

Viktor Frankl (1905–97) Austrian psychiatrist; Holocaust survivor who, out of his experience in Nazi death camps, developed his theory of logotherapy, which states that human motivation comes from a "will to meaning"; later became head of neurology at Vienna Polyclinic Hospital.

Benjamin Franklin (1706–90) American statesman, printer, writer, and scientist; one of the Founding Fathers and American representative in Paris; also a scientific innovator, particularly in electricity, and inventor of such devices as the lightning rod, bifocals, and the Franklin stove.

Robert Frost (1874–1963) American poet, known as "the voice of New England"; taught at Amherst College and Harvard; won the Pulitzer Prize three times, all for his characteristically terse "Yankee" verse.

R. Buckminister Fuller (1895–1983) American independent inventor who practiced what he preached—a dynamic lifestyle of invention; popularized his ideas of efficient living through his personally modified systems analysis; invented the geodesic dome.

Samuel Fuller (1912–97) American film director; decorated combat veteran, best known for grimly realistic war films, especially the 1980 classic *The Big Red One*; his journalistic style of filmmaking influenced later directors, including those of the French New Wave.

Mohandas K. Gandhi *(Mahatma)* (1869–1948) Indian spiritual and political leader, known as Mahatma (Great Soul); pioneered nonviolent resistance; regarded as a great politician and moral leader; led nonviolent civil disobedience movement against British rule in India; assassinated in 1948.

Janeane Garofalo (1964–) American actress and stand-up comedian; outspoken politically as a progressive activist.

Lou Gehrig (1903–41) American baseball player; New York Yankees power hitter and grand-slam record holder; nicknamed "The Iron Horse" for his strength and durability; died of amyotrophic lateral sclerosis (ALS), now known as Lou Gehrig's disease; announced he had the disease to a packed Yankee Stadium crowd, declaring that, despite this, he had been "the luckiest man on the face of the earth."

Geronimo (*Gokhlayeh: One Who Yawns*) (ca. 1829–1909) Apache chief; led his people in a series of uprisings (the Apache Wars of the 1880s); captured, escaped, and ultimately surrendered—and retired to farming in Oklahoma with the remnants of his people; dictated autobiography, *Geronimo, His Own Story*, in 1906.

Edward Gibbon (1737–94) British historian; best known for *The History of the Decline and Fall of the Roman Empire*, a massive, six-volume survey of Rome's decline that served as a model to later historians.

William S. Gilbert (1836–1911) British humourist, poet, and playwright; the "Gilbert" in light opera's famous Gilbert and Sullivan team; wrote fourteen popular comic operas with Arthur Sullivan, still widely performed and considered masterpieces.

Brendan Gill (1914–97) American writer and critic; wrote for *The New Yorker* magazine for over 60 years; champion of architectural preservation and other visual arts.

Natalie Goldberg (1948–) American writer; also writing teacher; integrates writing with Zen practice.

Graham Greene (1904–91) British writer; best known for his novels; work focused on moral issues from a Catholic perspective, often in exotic political settings; celebrated for lean, eminently readable literary style.

Wayne Gretzky (1961–) Canadian hockey player; rose to fame with the Edmonton Oilers, setting numerous scoring records and leading his team to four Stanley Cup Championships; credited with popularizing hockey in the U.S.

Dag Hammarskjöld (1905–61) Swedish statesman; served as second U.N. Secretary General; famed as activist peacemaker; died in mysterious circumstances in plane crash during a peace mission to the Congo; awarded the Nobel Peace Prize posthumously.

Samuel Hanagid (993–ca. 1055) Spanish-Hebrew poet; one of first Hebrew poets to write secular verse; ushered in golden age of Hebrew literature and arts.

Thomas Hardy (1840–1928) British poet and novelist; although best known today for his novels, considered himself a poet first; his celebrated regional novels—set in the fictional county of Wessex—reflect his sense of stoicism and the tragedy of human life.

Moss Hart (1904–61) American playwright and director; best known for his light 1930s' comedies, written in collaboration with friend George S. Kaufman; also wrote famous autobiography, *Act One*.

Bret Harte (ca. 1836–1902) American writer; noted for his "gold rush fiction," which celebrated the early rollicking days of the California gold rush, particularly in the classic *The Luck of Roaring Camp*.

Paul Harvey (1918–2009) American radio broadcaster; folksy, popular, and longtime broadcaster for ABC radio networks; his "News and Comment" and "The Rest of the Story" are heard by an estimated 22 million people worldwide.

Václav Havel (1936–) Czech statesman and writer; as a playwright and political dissident under Communist government, galvanized opposition to the state through his writings; later served as last president of Czechoslovakia and the first president of the Czech Republic.

Stephen Hawking (1942–) British physicist; known to the general public for popular books on cosmology; celebrated for contributions to theoretical physics in theorems of general relativity; almost completely paralyzed due to amyotrophic lateral sclerosis (ALS).

S. I. Hayakawa (*Samuel Ichiyé*) (1906–92) American senator and semanticist; Canadian born, became U.S.

citizen in 1955; wrote highly influential *Language in Thought and Action*; became president of San Francisco State University; served as U.S. Republican Senator from California from 1977 to 1983.

Heinrich Heine (1797–1856) German poet and journalist; one of most prominent of German romantic poets; lyrics have inspired such composers as Mendelssohn, Schubert, and Schumann.

Robert A. Heinlein (1907–88) American writer; called "the dean of science fiction writers"; wrote "hard science" fiction with many scientifically plausible speculations as well as political themes of freedom and sexual liberation; four-time Hugo Award winner.

Ernest Hemingway (1899–1961) American writer; known both for terse writing style and macho lifestyle; won Pulitzer Prize in 1953 for *The Old Man and the Sea* and the Nobel Prize in Literature in 1954.

Frank Herbert (1920–86) American writer; best known for his science fiction classic *Dune*, focusing on a desert planet and advanced ecology—one of the bestselling novels of all time, which spawned a series of related novels started by Herbert and continued by his son.

Hermann Hesse (1877–1962) German-Swiss writer and painter; wrote mystical novels that explore human spirituality, such as the acclaimed *Steppenwolf*,

Siddhartha, and *The Glass Bead Game (Magister Ludi)*; received Nobel Prize in Literature in 1946.

Tommy Hitchcock (1900–44) American polo player; considered greatest player of all time; flyer during World War I; basis for two F. Scott Fitzgerald characters; died testing airplane during World War II.

Eric Hoffer (1902–83) American writer/social commentator; focused on important role of self-esteem in human psyche; awarded Presidential Medal of Freedom in 1983.

Hugo von Hofmannsthal (1874–1929) Austrian novelist, poet, playwright, essayist, and librettist; collaborated with composer Richard Strauss on several operas, including *Der Rosenkavalier*.

Oliver Wendell Holmes Jr. (1841–1935) American judge and legal theorist; wrote definitive legal text on Common Law; served as associate justice of U.S. Supreme Court; one of the greatest legal figures of his time.

Lou Holtz (1937–) American football coach turned TV commentator and lecturer; led six different college teams to bowl games; member of the College Football Hall of Fame.

Horace *(Quintus Horatius Flaccus)* (65 B.C.– 8 B.C.) Roman poet; one of the greatest of the lyric poets from the golden age of Latin literature, under

Augustus Caesar; famed for his *Odes*, *Epodes*, *Satires*, and *Letters*.

Victor Hugo (1802–85) French poet and writer; a leader of the French romantic movement, best known for his panoramic social novel, *Les Miserables*; also active in French politics.

Jim "Catfish" Hunter (1946–99) American baseball pitcher; when playing with the Oakland Athletics in 1968, pitched the first perfect game in the American League since 1922; Cy Young Award winner; member of National Baseball Hall of Fame.

John Huston (1906–87) American director, actor, and screenwriter; famed for vibrant career and attitudes; directed *The Maltese Falcon*, *The Treasure of Sierra Madre*, and many other acclaimed films; died on location at age 81.

William Ralph Inge (1860–1954) English theologian and prelate, professor of divinity at Cambridge, later dean of St. Paul's; his pessimistic sermons earned him the nickname "the Gloomy Dean."

Christopher Isherwood (1904–86) British-born American novelist whose best-known works are based on his experiences in decadent pre-Hitler Berlin; *Berlin Stories* was basis for musical hit, *Cabaret*; later settled in California, worked as a screenwriter, translator, and novelist.

Molly Ivins (1944–2007) American columnist and political pundit; known for her scathingly humourous liberal commentary.

Mahalia Jackson (1911–72) One of America's leading gospel singers; three-time Grammy Award winner.

Jasper Johns Jr. (1930–) American artist; painter and printmaker; work considered among finest examples of American abstract expressionism and neo-Dadaism.

Samuel Johnson (1709–84) English writer and lexicographer; compiled the authoritative *Dictionary of the English Language* in 1755 and wrote numerous other works; was himself the subject of one of the most famous biographies in the English language, James Boswell's *Life of Samuel Johnson*.

Erica Jong (1942–) American novelist and poet; known for innovative style, attention to feminist issues; most famous work: *Fear of Flying*; active in fight for authors' rights; head of Authors Guild.

Michael Jordan (1963–) American basketball player; six-time NBA champion; called "Air Jordan"; considered by many to be the greatest basketball player of all time.

Juvenal (*Decimus Junius Juvenalis*) (ca. 60 A.D.– ca. 130) Roman satirist and lawyer celebrated for sixteen witty, acerbic satires in verse on Roman mores and vices; widely translated throughout history.

John Keats (1795–1821) English poet; leading member of the English romantics; noted for imagery and lyricism; odes are considered masterpieces of English literature.

Helen Keller (1880–1968) American writer and lecturer; blind and deaf after an illness at 19-months-old; became famous for having overcome her disabilities; lectured extensively and wrote numerous books including *The Story of My Life*; received the Presidential Medal of Freedom in 1967.

Walt Kelly (1913–73) American cartoonist; creator of the comic strip, *Pogo*, set in Georgia's Okefenokee Swamp; used strip for pointed political and social commentary, most notably against Senator Joe McCarthy; famous for the line, "We have met the enemy and he is us."

Thomas à Kempis (*Thomas Haemerkken*) (ca. 1380–1471) Medieval mystic and monk; member of the Augustinian Order; wrote mystical and devotional classic, *The Imitation of Christ*.

John F. Kennedy Jr. (1917–1963) American politician; hero during World War II; served as Massachusetts congressman and senator, then thirty-fifth president of the United States; youngest elected president as well as first (and only) Catholic; administration was known as Camelot for its idealism and youthful optimism; assassinated on November 22, 1963, in Dallas.

Jean Kerr (1922–2003) American writer; known for her humourous works about suburban family life, such as *Please Don't Eat the Daisies*, as well as her Broadway plays, such as *Mary, Mary*.

John Maynard Keynes (1883–1946) British economist; developed economic system now called Keynesian economics, emphasizing government fiscal and monetary intervention to keep economy stable.

Sue Monk Kidd (1948–) American writer; best known for her novels *The Secret Life of Bees* and *The Mermaid Chair*.

Søren Kierkegaard (1813–55) Danish philosopher and theologian; complex works emphasize religious themes and personal choices in life and combine elements of philosophy, theology, psychology, and literature.

Albert King (1923–92) American musician; blues guitarist and singer known as "the Velvet Bulldozer"; influenced rockers such as Eric Clapton and Jimi Hendrix.

Ernest J. King (1878–1956) American admiral; served as commander in chief, U.S. Fleet and chief of naval operations during World War II.

Elizabeth Kübler-Ross (1926–2004) American-Swiss psychiatrist; best known for her groundbreaking work on the personal aspects of death and dying; achieved worldwide acclaim for her first book, *On Death and Dying*.

Aung San Suu Kyi (1945–) Burmese (Myanmar) politician; leader of the National League for Democracy; advocates nonviolent resistance to tyranny; placed under house arrest in 1989; awarded Nobel Peace Prize in 1991.

Anne Lamott (1954–) American writer; best known for nonfiction semiautobiographical works.

Lao-zi *(Lao-tzu)* (ca. 604–c. 531 B.C.) Chinese philosopher; founder of Daoism; name literally means "old master"; his *Dao de Ching*, compiled 300 years after his death, teaches simplicity, detachment, going with the flow of nature.

Doug Larson (1926–) American journalist; wrote columns for the *Green Bay* (Wisconsin) *Press-Gazette* and the *Door County* (Wisconsin) *Advocate;* took over Bill Vaughn's humourous syndicated column "Senator Soaper Says" in 1980.

Tommy Lasorda (1927–) American baseball player and manager; spent twenty years as Los Angeles Dodgers manager, leading them to two World Series victories; inducted into National Baseball Hall of Fame in 1997.

Stephen Leacock (1869–1944) Canadian writer and economist; although head of the political economy department at McGill University, is best known for humour writing; between the years 1915 and 1925 was most popular humourist in the English-speaking world.

Fran Lebowitz (1950–) American humourist; known for acerbic short pieces on modern life.

Madeleine L'Engle (1918–2007) American writer of novels and children's books; won Newbery Award for children's classic, *A Wrinkle in Time.*

Sugar Ray Leonard (*Ray Charles Leonard*) (1956–) American boxer; one of boxing's all-time greats; named 1980s Fighter of the Decade.

Meridel Le Sueur (1900–96) American writer and activist; works focused on problems and struggles of the working classes and women's rights.

Primo Levi (1919–87) Italian writer and chemist; Auschwitz survivor who wrote haunting and acclaimed accounts of his experiences there; in addition to writing, continued chemical work; committed suicide in 1987.

C. S. Lewis (*Clive Staples*) (1898–1963) Anglo-Irish writer; Cambridge professor celebrated both for scholarly works on medieval literature and Christian works for adults (e.g., *The Screwtape Letters*) and children (e.g., *The Narnia Chronicles*).

Abraham Lincoln (1809–65) American statesman; sixteenth president of the United States; president during the Civil War; championed the Union and emancipation for slaves; assassinated while in office.

Jesse Livermore (1877–1940) American stock trader; known as "the Great Bear" due to his ability in "shorting" stocks in economic downturns, including the crash of 1929.

Livy (*Titus Livius*) (ca. 59 B.C.–ca. A.D. 17) Roman historian; wrote massive multivolume history of Rome—*Ab Urbe Condita* (*From the Founding*)—a principal source for modern knowledge of early Rome.

Vince Lombardi (1913–70) American football coach; spent nine years as head coach of Green Bay Packers, leading them to five NFL championships; known for his inspiring pep talks and "go-get 'em" demeanor.

Lone Man (*Isna-la-wica*) (1850–1918) Teton Sioux warrior; fought in Battle of Little Big Horn.

Huey P. Long (1893–1935) American politician; Louisiana governor and senator; nicknamed "the Kingfish," thanks, in part, to the motto "Every man a king"—from his Share Our Wealth redistribution program; assassinated in 1935.

Henry Wadsworth Longfellow (1807–82) American poet; professor of modern languages and literature at Harvard; gained great contemporary fame with romantic stories in verse, most notably *Hiawatha*.

James Russell Lowell (1819–91) American poet, editor, essayist, and diplomat; Harvard professor; advocated poetry as a tool in social reform; inspired H. L. Mencken and Mark Twain.

Martin Luther (1483–1546) German theologian; major church reformer; instigated the Protestant Reformation in Germany and neighbouring countries.

Lu Xun *(pseudonym of Chou Shu-jen)* (1881–1936) Chinese writer; considered to be the premier writer of his time and literary innovator for his vernacular style; most famous work is *Ah Q cheng-chuan* (*The True Story of Ah Q*).

Bill Maher (1956–) American comedian and television host; best known for sharp social commentary.

André Malraux (1901–76) French writer and intellectual; wrote groundbreaking book on Cambodian ruins; active in the Spanish Civil War and French Resistance; appointed French minister of information after World War II.

Nelson Mandela (1918–) African nationalist leader who opposed apartheid; sentenced to life imprisonment in 1964; became symbol of South African racist oppression; freed in 1990; in 1994 elected president of new multiracial South African government.

Katherine Mansfield (1888–1923) New Zealand writer; considered New Zealand's leading author; best known for modernist short stories.

José Martí (1853–95) Cuban patriot and writer; fought for Cuban independence; exiled and wrote chiefly in New York; founded Cuban Revolutionary Party; killed by Spanish after landing in Cuba to lead revolt.

Dean Martin (1917–95) American entertainer; singer, actor, television host, member of so-called Rat Pack with Sammy Davis Jr. and Frank Sinatra.

Groucho Marx *(Julius Henry)* (1890–1977) American writer, comedian, and actor; wisecracking member of the famed comedy team, the Marx Brothers; cowrote series of famous screenplays; later hosted a television show; wrote his autobiography, as well as a serious study of the income tax.

Jackie Mason (1931–) American comedian, known for rapid-fire borscht-belt style of humour.

H. L. Mencken (1880–1956) American journalist; known for humourous and acerbic attacks on American middle-class mores; wrote acclaimed study of American English.

Meng-tzu *(Mencius)* (ca. 371–ca. 289 B.C.) Chinese philosopher; considered a cofounder of Confucianism, as he developed and popularized the philosophy;

advocated social and political reform; after his death, his students collected his teachings and sayings.

A. A. Milne (1882–1956) English writer; famed for children's classic, *Winnie the Pooh*, and children's verse collections, such as *When We Were Very Young*.

Kenji Miyazawa (1896–1933) Japanese writer; noted as poet; acclaimed for works for children; as social activist, promoted peasants' rights.

Molière (*Jean-Baptiste Poquelin*) (1622–73) French playwright and actor; as head of acting troupe, wrote and produced masterpieces of French high comedy that exposed hypocrisy of French society, including *Le Misanthrope* (*The Misanthrope*).

Montesquieu (*Charles de Secondat, Baron de Montesquieu*) (1689-1755) French political theorist; best known for *Spirit of the Laws*, which advocated separation of powers.

Henry de Montherlant (1896–1972) French writer of essays and novels, but best known for plays; considered one of France's top twentieth-century playwrights.

J. P. Morgan (*John Pierpont*) (1837–1913) American financier, art collector, philanthropist; founded his own private bank, which became leading U.S. financial firm; almost single-handedly thwarted two stock-market panics.

Christopher Morley (1890–1957) American writer; a founder and longtime contributing editor of *Saturday Review of Literature*; wrote more than 100 books.

Toni Morrison (*Chloe Anthony Wofford*) (1931–) American novelist and memoirist; known for capturing African American experience, voice, and speech cadences; won Pulitzer Prize and Nobel Prize in Literature.

Lewis Mumford (1895–1990) American urban historian and writer; wrote extensively on cities, architecture; opposed massive urban projects in favour of more human-oriented development; called by Malcolm Cowley "the last of the great humanists."

Paul Newman (1925–2008) American actor, director, humanitarian; noted award-winning actor for gritty roles in films such as *Cool Hand Luke* and *The Color of Money*; cofounded charitable food company.

Randy Newman (1943–) American musician; singer and songwriter noted for pointed songs about the American experience; also known for Academy Award–winning film scores.

Michel Ney, Duc d'Elchingen (1769–1815) French soldier; Napoleonic marshal of the army; commanded the Old Guard at the Battle of Waterloo; executed by restored Bourbon monarchy.

Flannery O'Connor (1925–64) American short-story writer and novelist; known for black-humoured stories of the South; recipient of National Book Award; famous works include *Wise Blood* and *A Good Man Is Hard to Find*.

George Orwell (*Eric Arthur Blair*) (1903–50) English writer; fought in Spanish Civil War; best known for antitotalitarian novels *Animal Farm* and *Nineteen Eighty-Four*.

Osceola (ca. 1803–38) Seminole chief; prominent leader of Second Seminole War of 1835–42; taken prisoner while under flag of truce; later died of an illness in a cell at Fort Moultrie, Georgia.

William Osler (1849–1919) Canadian physician; called the "most influential physician in history" and "the father of modern medicine," owing to pioneering of hands-on medical residency for medical students.

Leroy "Satchel" Paige (1906–82) American baseball star; pitched for Negro Leagues and major leagues; the oldest rookie to play major-league baseball—and, at age 59, the oldest man to pitch in a major-league game; member of National Baseball Hall of Fame.

Thomas Paine (1737–1809) British-born American revolutionary and writer; wrote the incendiary pamphlet, *Common Sense*, in 1776, which inspired

American colonists to revolt; his later *Rights of Man* had great influence on the French Revolution.

Blaise Pascal (1623–62) French mathematician, physicist, and religious philosopher; made important contributions in conic sections and projective geometry; helped lay foundations for the theory of probability; religious ascetic and mystic.

Boris Pasternak (1890–1960) Russian novelist and poet; best known in the West for his epic about life in the early Soviet Union, *Doctor Zhivago*, and in Russia for his poetry, particularly for his influential *My Sister—Life*.

Thomas J. Pendergast (1872–1945) political boss of Kansas City and Jackson County, Missouri; controlled politicians and doled out political favours; assisted Harry S Truman in his early career.

Laurence J. Peter (1919–90) Canadian American educator; best known for the Peter Principle, which states: "In a hierarchy every employee tends to rise to his level of incompetence."

William Pitt the Younger (1759–1806) British statesman; became England's youngest prime minister at age 24; served in this office twice; notable for rallying Britain against Napoleon.

Plautus (*Titus Maccius Plautus*) (ca. 254–ca. 184 B.C.) Roman playwright; known for comedies based on Hellenistic Greek originals, but with a uniquely

Roman vigor and bawdiness; influenced playwrights from Shakespeare to the present.

Pliny the Younger *(Gaius Plinius Caecilius Secundus)* (ca. 61–ca. 113) Roman writer and statesman; best known for *Letters*, which reveal the life of a wealthy gentleman in ancient Rome.

Pythagoras (ca. 580–ca. 500 B.C.) Greek mathematician and philosopher; sometimes called "the first pure mathematician"; incorporated his mathematical ideas into his mystical philosophy.

François Rabelais (ca. 1494–ca. 1553) French writer and doctor; leading figure during the Renaissance; known as one of the great comic geniuses of literature; employed the grotesque and the bawdy in his work.

Tunku Abdul Rahman Putra (1903–90) Malaysian prime minister; presided over decolonisation of Malaysia after British rule; reduced tensions between the country's Chinese and Malay ethnic groups.

Ramakrishna *(Gadadhar Chatterjee)* (1833–86) Indian mystic; leading Tantrist teacher; evolved theory that all religions are different paths to same goal.

Jeanette Rankin (1880–1973) American congresswoman; first woman to join the U.S. House of Representatives; first winner of National Organization of Women's Susan B. Anthony Award.

Pierre-Auguste Renoir (1841–1919) French artist; one of the leaders of the impressionists; best known for soft-focus female nudes and other sensual subjects.

Jacob A. Riis (1849–1914) Danish American journalist and photographer; a leading muckraker and social reformer; photo essays of New York City tenement life helped bring about housing reforms; flash-photography innovator.

Luis Muñoz Rivera (1859–1916) Puerto Rican journalist and politician; funded newspaper *La Democracia*; campaigned for Puerto Rican independence; held range of government positions.

Jackie Robinson (1919–72) American baseball player; first athlete to break color barrier in major-league baseball as star player for Brooklyn Dodgers; elected to National Baseball Hall of Fame in 1962.

Will Rogers (1879–1935) American humourist and performer; known for down-home social commentary; became top-paid Hollywood star in mid-1930s; was killed during an around-the-world airplane trip with aviator Wiley Post.

Franklin D. Roosevelt (1882–1945) American politician, thirty-second president of the U.S.; considered one of the most influential U.S. presidents, for New Deal policies during Great

Depression; mobilised the U.S. against fascism during World War II; the only president to have served more than two terms.

Theodore Roosevelt (1858–1919) American politician, twenty-sixth president of the U.S.; also served as governor of New York; known for his energetic and vigorous personality; besides his work in politics, wrote numerous books, sponsored and participated in scientific expeditions, hunted, and soldiered.

Billy Rose (1899–1966) American theater impresario and lyricist; owned and operated famed Diamond Horseshoe nightclub and the Ziegfeld and Billy Rose Theatres; wrote many hit songs, including "Me and My Shadow" and "It's Only a Paper Moon."

Nathaniel Mayer Victor Rothschild, 3rd Baron Rothschild (1910–90) British biologist and cricket player; member of the famed Rothschild banking family.

J. K. Rowling (1965–) British writer; famed for her Harry Potter series about a young wizard, which has sold more than 400 million copies worldwide.

Rumi (*Jalil ad-Din*) (1207–73) Sufi poet; one of the most influential Sufi leaders and mystic poets; founded Mevlevi Order of dervishes.

Damon Runyon (1884–1946) American writer and newsman; wrote popular tales of Broadway tough guys, gamblers, gangsters, and showgirls—later adapted for the musical *Guys and Dolls.*

Bertrand Russell (1872–1970) British philosopher; wrote landmark work on logic and mathematics, *Principia Mathematica*, as well as epistemological works; active in political and social causes.

Rosalind Russell (1907–76) American actress; successful both in film and on stage; known for roles such as the fast-talking Hildy in *His Girl Friday* and the irrepressible Auntie Mame.

Babe Ruth *(George Herman Ruth)* (1895–1948) American baseball player; began as a pitcher, but achieved fame as a home-run slugger; arguably the best player in baseball history; called "the Bambino" and "the Sultan of Swat."

Antoine de Saint Exupéry (1900–44) French writer and pilot; best known for sweetly philosophical novella, *The Little Prince*, and his lyrical accounts of flying; shot down in combat over France in 1944.

J. D. Salinger (1919–) American novelist and short-story writer; wrote modern classic novel about youthful angst, *The Catcher in the Rye*; known for extremely reclusive lifestyle.

Sivananda Saraswati (1887–1963) Indian businessman and religious leader; founded the

Divine Life Society and the University at the Forest; advocated simple Vedanta-oriented philosophy.

Virginia Satir (1916–88) American psychologist and educator; best known for family therapy work and "change process model" of analysis.

Charles M. Schulz (1922–2000) American cartoonist; creator of the ever-popular comic strip, *Peanuts*, which captures the woes and wonders of childhood.

Albert Schweitzer (1875–1965) Alsatian missionary, theologian, musician, and philosopher; founded (and built) hospital in what was then French Equatorial Africa; awarded the Nobel Peace Prize in 1952 for his "reverence for life" philosophy.

Maurice Sendak (1928–) American writer and illustrator; best known for his whimsical children's works, such as *Where the Wild Things Are*.

Seneca (*Lucius Annaeus Seneca*) (ca. 4 B.C.– ca. A.D. 65) Roman Stoic philosopher and tragic playwright; tutor to Roman emperor Nero, whom he tried to influence for the better, but was condemned by his student; committed suicide.

William Shakespeare (1564–1616) English playwright and poet; called "the Bard of Avon"; widely considered the English-speaking world's leading dramatist, whose plays have been performed more than those of any other writer.

George Bernard Shaw (1856–1950) Anglo-Irish playwright, critic, essayist, political activist; member of the socialist Fabian Society, but best known for his vigorous, acerbic plays, such as *Man and Superman* and *Pygmalion*; winner of the Nobel Prize in Literature.

William Tecumseh Sherman (1820–91) American soldier; as Union Civil War general, distinguished himself as military strategist but was often criticised for "scorched earth" total war methods; aptly noted that "war is hell."

Shingis (Eighteenth century) Delaware chief during French and Indian War; forced into alliance with French by Chief Pontiac.

Isaac Bashevis Singer (1904–91) Polish-born American writer; won Nobel Prize in Literature for his poignant novels and short stories, all written in Yiddish, chronicling Jewish life in Poland and U.S.

Sitting Bull (*Tatanka Iyotake*) (ca. 1831–90) Dakota Sioux chief and medicine man; led his tribe in Black Hills War of 1876–77 and the Battle of Little Big Horn; toured with Buffalo Bill's Wild West show; killed on North Dakota reservation by U.S. army officer.

Amarillo Slim (*Thomas Austin Preston Jr.*) (1928–) American professional poker player; winner of the prestigious World Series of Poker "main event"; member of the Poker Hall of Fame.

Dodie Smith (1896–1990) English novelist and playwright; wrote children's classic, *The One Hundred and One Dalmatians*.

Socrates (469–399 B.C.) Greek philosopher, mentor to Plato; although he wrote nothing, his ideas as reported by Plato form one of the foundations of Western philosophy; ordered to commit suicide by drinking hemlock as a punishment for "corrupting the young" and encouraging them to question the political and social values of the day.

George Soros (1930–) Hungarian-born investor and philanthropist; famous for betting against the British pound in 1992—garnering himself 1.1 billion dollars and the nickname "the Man Who Broke the Bank of England"; principally known today for philanthropy and dedication to liberal political causes.

Bruce Springsteen (1949–) American rock musician; nicknamed "the Boss"; work often focuses on problems and struggles of the lower and middle classes, particularly in his home state of New Jersey; winner of eighteen Grammy awards.

Gertrude Stein (1874–1946) American writer and critic; influenced contemporary artists; applied theories of abstract art to writing.

John Steinbeck (1902–68) American writer; known especially for novels and short fiction focusing on the poor and downtrodden, such as *Of Mice and Men* and the iconic *The Grapes of Wrath*; won the Nobel Prize in Literature.

Casey Stengel (1890–1975) American baseball player and manager; played with Brooklyn Dodgers, then managed the New York Yankees and led them to seven World Series victories; later managed the New York Mets; famous for colorful and unique way of speaking.

Robert Louis Stevenson (1850–94) Scottish writer; wrote poems, essays, fiction, and travel books; best known for romantic adventure stories such as *Treasure Island* and *Kidnapped*; beginning in late 1880s, lived with his family on the South Sea island of Samoa.

Publilius Syrus (First century B.C.) Roman writer; born in Assyria and brought to Italy as a slave; freed and educated by his master who was impressed by his talent; chiefly known for pithy maxims.

Rabindranath Tagore (1861–1941) Indian poet, novelist, and philosopher; founded school seeking to blend Eastern and Western philosophies and educational systems; won Nobel Prize in Literature.

Tecumseh (ca. 1768–1813) Shawnee chief; organizer of Indian confederation and leader of Tecumseh's Rebellion of 1809–11.

Teresa of Avila (*née Teresa de Cepeda y Ahumada*) (1515–82) Spanish mystic, nun, and poet; founded nine convents; Carmelite Order reformer; co-patron saint of Spain.

Mother Teresa (*Agnes Gonxha Bojaxhiu*) (1910–99) Albanian Roman Catholic nun and humanitarian; famed for her sisterhood dedicated to helping the world's poorest, most notably in Calcutta, India; won Nobel Peace Prize in 1979.

Nancy Thayer (1943–) Nantucket-based American novelist; works revolve around relationships and family dynamics.

Henry David Thoreau (1817–62) American naturalist, writer, activist, and transcendentalist; best known for philosophy of civil disobedience, elucidated in his essay *Civil Disobedience* as well as in his famous book *Walden* about solitary life at Walden Pond.

James Thurber (1894–1961) American humourist, cartoonist, and writer; famed contributor to *The New Yorker* magazine; wrote fiction, fables, short stories, essays as well as captions for his own cartoons.

Mike Todd (*Avrom Hirsch Goldbogen*) (1909–58) American film and theatre producer; won a Best

Picture Oscar for *Around the World in Eighty Days*; known as technical innovator in filmmaking.

Leo Tolstoy (1828–1910) Russian writer and moralist; most famous for masterpieces *War and Peace* and *Anna Karenina*; a pioneer of the psychological novel; fought in Crimean War, which inspired his antiwar attitudes; at the end of his life, turned over his fortune to his wife and lived as a peasant.

Desmond Tutu (1931–) South African clergyman and activist; gained worldwide fame as fighter against apartheid; awarded Nobel Peace Prize, Albert Schweitzer Prize for Humanitarianism, and Gandhi Peace Prize.

Mark Twain (*Samuel Langhorne Clemens*) (1835–1910) American writer; wrote classics such as *Tom Sawyer* and *Huckleberry Finn*, accounts drawn from his own boyhood; the preeminent American humourist and satirist of the nineteenth century.

Ernestine Ulmer (1925–) American writer.

Peter Ustinov (1921–2004) British actor and writer; directed theatre and opera, designed sets, wrote for newspapers and magazines, lectured and appeared frequently as a guest and presenter on television shows.

Queen Victoria (1819–1901) British queen; longest ruling monarch of Great Britain; ruled during the height of the British Empire; added India among other colonies to her dominion so that Britain controlled one-quarter of the globe.

Paul Volcker (1927–) American economist; former chairman of the Federal Reserve under presidents Jimmy Carter and Ronald Reagan; famed for his deft handling of the economy and reining in inflation; head of President Obama's Economic Recovery Advisory Board.

François–Marie Arouet Voltaire (1694–1778) French philosopher and writer; principal champion of the European Enlightenment; wrote scathing satires, most notably *Candide*, which lampooned the optimistic philosopher Leibniz.

Kurt Vonnegut Jr. (1922–2007) American writer; best known for his groundbreaking comedic science fiction, which garnered cult following in 1960s, including *Slaughterhouse-Five*, inspired by the Allied bombing of Dresden.

Alice Walker (1944–) American novelist and poet; writing influenced by African American speech patterns in the South and tradition of storytelling; winner of American Book Award and Pulitzer Prize for *The Color Purple*.

John Wayne (*Marion Morrison*) (1907–79) American film actor; called "Duke"; the archetype of

American masculinity; particularly known for starring roles in Westerns and war movies.

Orson Welles (1915–85) American film director, producer, writer, and actor; best known for earlier work, including attention-grabbing radio presentation of Martian invasion, "The War of the Worlds," and the consistently voted "best film of all time," *Citizen Kane*.

J. A. Wheeler (1911–2008) American theoretical physicist; collaborated with Albert Einstein; most famous for coining the words "black hole" and "wormhole."

E. B. White (1899–1985) American writer; especially known for classic children's works, *Charlotte's Web* and *Stuart Little*; also acclaimed for contributions to *The New Yorker* magazine, most notably essays and "Notes and Comments."

Oscar Wilde (1854–1900) Irish writer; famous as trendsetting aesthete and wit as well as popular Victorian playwright, most notably for *The Importance of Being Earnest*; found guilty of "gross indecency" for sexual activities with other men; was sent to Reading Gaol for two years, where he wrote acclaimed *Ballad of Reading Gaol*.

Oprah Winfrey (1954–) American media mogul and philanthropist; born in poverty in rural Mississippi;

rose to host of highest-rated talk show in television history; has won numerous Emmys; credited with reviving interest in reading by featuring selected books on her show.

Alexander Woollcott (1887–1943) American critic and commentator; key member of famed Algonquin Roundtable and frequent contributor to *The New Yorker* magazine; celebrated for acerbic wit.

Frank Lloyd Wright (1867–1959) American architect with bold, innovative style; completed the Guggenheim Museum in New York at age 91.

Xi Zhi (*Hsün-Tzu*) (ca. 303–361 B.C.) Chinese neo-Confucian philosopher, diametrically opposed to that of Mencius (Meng-tzu); emphasized that human nature is originally evil and that social control must be employed.

About the Authors

Kathryn and **Ross Petras**, sister-and-brother quotation connoisseurs, have published numerous collections of their finds, including *Age Doesn't Matter Unless You're a Cheese.* They live with their families in New York and New Jersey.